SMALL-SCALE
HOMESTEADING

SMALL-SCALE HOMESTEADING

A Sustainable Guide to Gardening, Keeping Chickens, Maple Sugaring, Preserving the Harvest, and More

STEPHANIE THUROW & MICHELLE BRUHN

Skyhorse Publishing

We acknowledge that we're writing on Indigenous Dakota and Lakota lands. By offering this land acknowledgment, we affirm tribal sovereignty and express respect for Native peoples and nations. We are on the ancestral lands of the Dakota people. We want to acknowledge the Dakota, the Ojibwe, the Ho Chunk, and the other nations of people who also called this place home. We are grateful for the knowledge Indigenous peoples have gathered and continue to share with us. We urge you to explore the rich history and current Indigenous activism of your local community.

Skyhorse Publishing books may be purchased in bulk at special discounts for sales promotion, corporate gifts, fund-raising, or educational purposes. Special editions can also be created to specifications. For details, contact the Special Sales Department, Skyhorse Publishing, 307 West 36th Street, 11th Floor, New York, NY 10018 or info@skyhorsepublishing.com.

Skyhorse® and Skyhorse Publishing® are registered trademarks of Skyhorse Publishing, Inc.®, a Delaware corporation.

Visit our website at www.skyhorsepublishing.com.

10 9 8 7 6 5 4 3 2 1

Library of Congress Cataloging-in-Publication Data is available on file.

Cover design by David Ter-Avanesyan
Cover images by Stephanie Thurow & Michelle Bruhn

Print ISBN: 978-1-5107-7036-2
Ebook ISBN: 978-1-5107-7037-9

Printed in China

Dedicated to my Sophia. Love, Mom

Dedicated to my boys, Toby + Foster, I love you.

TABLE OF CONTENTS

INTRODUCTION TO HOMESTEADING

Welcome to the wonderful world of homesteading— we're so glad you're here! Pull up a chair, grab a cup of tea or coffee, and savor these pages at your own pace. We'll be right here waiting for you.

Homesteading is part of a larger movement that encompasses eating local, climate action, and forging a closer relationship with nature and our families. With the proven benefits of spending time in nature mounting, along with the fact that fresh, organic food is better for us and the economies of our communities—not to mention way more delicious—thinking and acting in a homesteading mindset, wherever you are, is a natural next step. We know because we've been on the same wild ride as you!

Hi, we're Stephanie and Michelle, two Minnesota moms who fell in love with homesteading in very different ways, but found friendship through our shared passions for real, local food and our DIY hearts.

Come along as we share what (and who) has helped us live a little closer to nature—without giving up our neighborhoods. Rather, we'll share how our communities and the bountiful resources right around the corner have helped us live a more authentic garden-to-table lifestyle. We've curated our favorite skills, tips, tricks, and the inspirations behind them in this book just for you.

From growing more of your own food, harvesting and preserving like a pro, making your own maple syrup and soap, to collecting that first egg from your backyard flock, we offer the skills to help you live like a true modern-day homesteader.

We believe wholeheartedly that any home can be a homestead!

Chapter One

OUR HOMESTEAD STORIES

Michelle's Homesteading Story

Our suburban homestead took root in a home we thought we were going to flip fifteen years ago. So now, even though the idea of the back forty still holds some allure, we're abundantly content. Our journey has followed our family's changing passions and curiosities, keeping centered on the larger goal of living more in sync with mother nature and our community.

But it wasn't always like that. I used to work in marketing and eat microwavable lunches five days a week. Having kids, becoming aware of all the toxicity in everyday products, and abruptly quitting said job led me down such a beautiful and bumpy (and dirty, *definitely* dirty) road that now I can't imagine life any other way!

What started as a rekindling of my love of gardening turned quickly into preserving, raising chickens, making soap, sourdough, and countless other projects. One thing led to another, and I started writing about the way I was growing food and the farmers I was meeting on my local food escapades. Then I created my website, *Forks in the Dirt*, to share those stories. Soon I had started a winter farmers' market to help bring my neighbors and local food together even in the depths of Minnesota winters.

I love being immersed in many different projects all at once, so our home is always a space "in process." There are usually herbs hanging to dry and mason jars bubbling away with ferments on the counters. Winter finds wood chips on the floor and smoke-scented hair as I tend our wood stove and cook from our pantry of preserves. In the spring there are trays of seedlings on every available surface. Summer means long days in the gardens and baskets of just harvested food crowding the counters waiting to be eaten or preserved. Fall brings curing onions and squash, and seeds stashed in every corner.

And then there's the backyard. Our ever-evolving vegetable gardens, wood piles, compost piles, the chicken coop, the pollinator gardens . . . and in all that chaos we find such peace!

Last year our family grew around six hundred pounds of nutrient-dense produce from our gardens. Add in almost enough eggs for our family of four, plus maple syrup to nearly see us through the year, herbs to flavor, and tea to savor—yes, we're proud of our little homestead's abundance. But we enjoy our local farmer friends and what they provide (both in products and personality) way too much to strive to separate from that. It is also illegal to have hooved animals in many cities and suburbs, so our milk and bacon has to come from somewhere else.

Don't forget about buying meat and dairy products from your local farmers, like Brian of KDE Farms, as well. Grass-fed beef, pastured hogs, plus milk and cheeses from well-loved animals tastes better and is better for you!

Stephanie's Homesteading Story

Fifteen years ago, we purchased our current home in a first-ring suburb of Minneapolis. Our home sits on a .18-acre lot. For years I dreamed of moving out of the city to a quiet rural area with acres of land and rolling hills. I imagined it would have orchards of fruit trees and space to grow and raise as much food as our hearts desired. I envisioned goats and chickens, with plenty of room to roam. But I grew up in south Minneapolis in Minnesota and so did my husband. We were used to city life and its many conveniences, plus most of our family and friends are here.

With the birth of our daughter came my concern and desire for a healthy home. I abruptly became aware of the harmful ingredients in everyday products, such as our lotion and cleaning products. I suddenly cared immensely about the food we ate and the quality of what we consumed. I began to make as much as I could from scratch. Before I knew it, we were making our own lotion, yogurt, candles, cleaning products, bug spray, and so much more.

I'd already been preserving my own food for many years before my daughter was born, but during those years, I'd bought most of the produce I canned from farmers. As my daughter grew, so did her love of helping in the garden, so we kept expanding our garden space annually. She still eats the majority of our cherry tomatoes and rattlesnake pole beans even to this day, a decade later. My daughter's fascination with the garden (and all the critters found within) sparked something inside me and it suddenly felt much more important to do even more with what we had—initially for her, but ultimately for all of us, for our family.

Though our actual growing space is not very large, by utilizing it properly we've been able to grow several hundreds of pounds of food each year, tap our maple trees to make more than enough delicious pure maple syrup for the year, plus raise a small flock of laying hens that produce over eight hundred eggs a year, and we still have plenty of room for the dogs and children to play.

It's hard to put into words the satisfaction I get from making delicious meals for those I love most, with ingredients that have largely come from either my front or back yard. The flavor of freshly harvested homegrown food is incomparable to anything from the grocery store. Not to mention that the fruits and vegetables are so much more nutritious when eaten fresh. And growing food yourself is much more affordable.

That all being said, I'm still very much a city gal. I order from Instacart weekly and very much enjoy the convenience of the airport being a ten-minute drive from home. But I think it's important to understand that a lot can be done, even without a lot of space. Not everything has to be done at once, either. Take your time, expand on your skills annually, and do what physically, mentally, and economically works for you and your family.

Homestead Frame of Mind

We see our homes as a place of production, not just consumption.

When we realize that we're part of the natural world out our back door, not separate from it, we start seeing how interconnected it all is. When we come into relationship with nature, we take better care of nature.

So, in our families, as in this book, we measure success in different metrics than you might expect. Yes, we want to grow lots of food, and we do, but true success comes from working together, learning new skills, being outside, and enjoying the process. When you look at it that way, homesteading becomes an adventure!

Extending beyond our own yard, we are also dedicated to being part of our local community. We love our local farmers, farmers' markets, community gardens, schoolyard gardens, and actively participate in those to both learn from and give back to our neighbors.

MICHELLE

Even when I lived on a large farm in Sweden, we still depended on our neighboring farms—one for milk and the other for pork. We had a flour mill, and the best potato planting and moose hunting land. So, we offered that to the community, and received other products and services in return. We also shared the most picturesque roadside root cellar. The key was working together.

Sharing the Skills

The idea of working together is integral to small-scale homesteading. We can each do what our land, our talents, and interests lend themselves to within this enticing homesteading world. Just as importantly, leave what doesn't spark joy for you to your neighbors. Letting someone else flourish and share their skills and bounty with the community is a gift to them as well.

To this end, we've both taught classes on canning and fermenting (Stephanie) or gardening and composting (Michelle). This book combines our knowledge, joy, and step-by-step DIY all in one place. This book is like a big ol' smorgasbord table laid out for you to enjoy and return to as you become hungry for the next step in your homesteading journey. This book is not a comprehensive guide to all things homesteading. It's a book about what *we* do and how we do it

and what works for us, and we hope that you learn from our experience (and mistakes) to do more with what you have, too.

On that note, we are far from self-sufficient, and that is not our goal. **We are far more interested in living sustainably in community than sufficiently by ourselves.** We are gathering skills that help us survive, but we thrive when we share our skills with others.

We think it's unsustainable to be self-sufficient on the average urban or suburban lot. I know there are books that claim to tell you how to do it. But for most of us, we'd never be able to make that work, let alone sustain it. For our families, the amount of effort to make self-sufficiency happen on ⅛ to ½ an acre isn't worth the neglect of other life experiences. Maybe we can turn the idea of homesteading on its head. **Instead of self-sufficiency, how about communal abundance?**

You'll find both the why and the how for many small-scale homesteading opportunities throughout the following pages so you can find what works for you. We hope it also inspires you to find your locals who are thriving at different aspects of homesteading. This is your free pass to pick your own path and dig into (only) what you love.

Know Your Farmer

One of my biggest aha moments on my homesteading journey was when I realized I really didn't have to grow it all. Leaning on my local farmers has done more for my garden than anything else. Why? Because as I got to know my farmers better, I started trusting them to grow my family's food. It took away the pressure to perform, and instead opened doors to community and relationships! For me, that was a

Many local farms (like All Good Organics here) operate their own on-site farm stores. This allows farmers to offer the freshest produce, plants, and goods without traveling to farmers' markets multiple days a week. I love this option for both farmers and those looking to buy local!

total game changer. I stopped letting perfect get in the way of good!

Shopping farmers' markets gives you a great opportunity to get to know your farmer while seeing what is in season in your area. This kind of shopping differs from shopping at the grocery store, so let's take advantage of those differences. They're also a great place to sample new veggies, delicious cheeses, and new cuts of humanely raised meats as well! Food is fun, and farmers' markets are wonderful at reminding us of that!

When people see firsthand how much time, knowledge, and physical effort goes into growing food, they are much less likely to waste it. Buying local or growing our own helps us value our food more and waste it less. On page 22, we go over how to make it easy and sustainable to compost on your homestead!

It Takes Family + Community

Making your home a safe place to make a mess and make mistakes is essential to growing together as a family. There are lots of different ways to get your kids involved but the main thing is to allow them to keep trying and to see you keep trying and learning from your mistakes. Building a bird house, keeping bird feeders and bird baths full, raising monarch butterflies, and planting for pollinators are all ways kids can care for nature right out their back door. If they see you having fun in the garden or kitchen, they'll want to be in on it, too. Trust us.

STEPHANIE

What about people who don't have space to grow food, raise chickens, or store cases of canned goods? My answer is to work together. Many cities have community garden plots that can be reserved for personal growing. If your city doesn't have one yet, perhaps that is something you can implement. Or maybe there is a neighbor nearby that does have growing space in their yard, but they only use it to grow grass. Working together, you could transform an otherwise plain grassy yard into an urban garden plot to share.

Consider a trade of skills with other locals. By working together, goals can be met and it's a whole lot easier (and more fun) than doing it all alone. Take this book—it's a perfect example of combining strengths to reach a common goal.

There is such a beautiful opportunity for everyone to see their current situation as a perfect starting point. You can help the environment, eat better, and raise amazing down-to-earth kids all within whatever space you already have. There is power in your landscape choices, your meal choices, and all the things you bring into your home. Taking hold of that power is better for your health, the health and economy of our communities, and the planet. We're blending modern life with the simple life. Garden to table and eco-minimalism. Backyard chickens with front yard gardens. All with our communities at hand and in mind.

We're all in this together.
Let's dig in,

Stephanie & Michelle

URBAN FARMING
Jade and Carrie
The Black Radish CSA
@theblackradish_
Minneapolis, Minnesota

Urban farmers and artists, Carrie and Jade, learned the importance of healthy soil and growing food as children. Together in 2018, they began The Black Radish CSA at their urban homestead. They provide an assortment of healthy, affordable, organic food to their community. Over the years, they have turned their front and back yards from ornamental lawn to productive garden space, as well as ten of their neighbors' lawns. What an inspiration!

Homeowners that transform their lawns receive a free CSA subscription and don't have to do any of the work. "It's amazing how many people really don't want to mow and would prefer to see their front yard turned into a functioning garden that feeds not only them, but others as well," Jade and Carrie explained. They believe that their neighbors participate because it is a real way to connect with their community and it brings about a positive change that they can see and really be a part of. Their advice to those interested in growing food instead of grass: "Start small and don't be afraid of things not growing, because sometimes they don't. Add on

more each year, learn more. Instant gratification is not part of farming; it's more of a slow meditation."

I am happiest when in my garden and I can't wait for you to find that same joy—plus dig into all the benefits of growing more of your own food! You've heard our stories about how we ended up homesteading in our own ways, but there's a movement that has people from all over the globe heading back to their gardens, too.

Today's gardeners are growing in awareness that they can feed their families, help pollinators, and regenerate the soil—all at the same time. While each garden will be as unique as the gardener digging it in, growing food brings us together in so many ways. By growing more food in whatever space we have, we're making a difference.

Community gardens continue to sprout up all over the country. Garden clubs and organizations are bursting with new gardeners and dedicated mentors. Regardless of where you fall on the garden love level, there is a place for you on the path. Keeping in mind what *your* goals are from the beginning will help you (quite literally) stay grounded.

The longer you garden the more you'll become aware that biodiversity equals strength in the garden just like a wide diversity of people equals strength in our communities.

Permaculture at a Glance

As any gardener will tell you, working with nature is much easier and more rewarding than working against it. Permaculture invites you to look at what your yard already has and make good use of it. Planting self-supporting guilds (a group of plants that help each other grow better) of plants is encouraged. Permaculture also divides yards into zones, with the area closest to your home as zone 1, and concentric circles reaching out to the edges of your yard. If this way of gardening interests you, we recommend the classic book *Gaia's Garden: A Guide to Home-Scale Permaculture* by Toby Hemenway.

KNOW YOUR HARDINESS ZONE!

The USDA produces a useful gardening guide showing different growing zones based on temperature (see on page 131). Match plants to your zone for the best success!

SUNLIGHT

Most vegetables want a minimum of eight hours and thrive with a full ten or more hours of sunlight. You can't alter hours of sunlight without removing some trees so I suggest "sun mapping" to start you off. Sun mapping involves staking out where you want the garden and taking note every hour how many hours of sunlight that spot gets. This eliminates the mistake of trying to grow vegetables where you only get three hours of sun. Bonus points if you do this a few months apart as you will appreciate how drastically the angle of the sun changes during the seasons.

WATER AWARENESS

Locating your garden near a water source makes good sense. Think about how you'll drag a hose through garden paths if needed when planning the layout of garden beds. Personally, I enjoy hand watering and find that it's a great way to stay in tune with my plants. I often catch insect infestations and diseased plants early because I hand water but installing an irrigation system is another option for some and can be a great way to save water and time tending your garden.

ELEVATION

Is the garden location on high or low ground? This (combined with soil type) could mean a soggy, waterlogged garden bed, or one that quickly dries out. There are ways to work around this with terracing of steep hills, creating swales to hold water, and drainage paths to let water run away from low-lying areas. Mountaintop elevations will have to pay closer attention to their own weather cycles for temperatures.

WILDLIFE

Take some time to observe the signs of wildlife, from scat to scratch marks, paths, and patterns. For example, squirrels frequent the ground below bird feeders, while rabbits love to hang out under dense shrubs. Think twice if you're planning a garden in the middle of a wildlife highway.

PRO BACKYARD BIRDING TIP

By placing a bird bath and a bird feeder across the yard from each other you can create a flight pattern tailored to your viewing spots for more bird watching fun! Thanks to Don Engebretson, "The Renegade Gardener," for sharing this tip years ago!

PLANNING A VEGETABLE GARDEN

Before we dig into designing your garden, take a step back and ask yourself why you want to grow a garden. What are your goals? Is it about eating fresh during the summer, preserving food for the winter, cutting costs by growing what's most expensive in the stores, or creating a space for your family to all work together? Whatever your goal, it is valid and worthy of your time—and not to be compared to anyone else's!

Grow what you love. Think about your favorite family meals, or what you love to buy fresh from the farmers' markets; the plants that make up those memories are what you should grow first. Start gathering a list of the fruits and vegetables you most want to grow.

COMMUNITY GARDENING

If you have a less than perfect yard for growing food, consider bartering with a neighbor to grow in their space and split the produce, or focus on herbs and salad greens from your shady yard. There are many varieties of community gardens, from small urban plots alongside an apartment complex to suburban church landscapes. Community gardens come with the bonus of working alongside other knowledgeable gardeners.

We've got a mix of berry bushes, perennial flowers, and annual squash vines growing in our front yard garden.

Site Considerations

Consider both your front and backyard for growing food. It is becoming more and more common for urban and suburban yards to contain edible plantings in the front yard (yay!). There is something so engaging about adding a garden to the public-facing side of your yard. My front yard garden has helped me meet neighbors, start friendships, and pet lots of dogs! I've also exchanged plants, ideas, and garden love from people I never would have met if I was tucked away in my backyard. That said, I also adore the privacy and seclusion I experience being lost in my backyard gardens. Consider the best location for you and what you want to grow.

BEFORE YOU DIG

Your local city ordinances may have setbacks from roads and property lines for gardens, sheds, and sometimes even fences (sorry, corner lots). Make a quick call to your city ahead of time, and homeowner's association if you have one, before digging into the ground. The national **#811 "Call Before You Dig"** hotline is essential! This is the number to call to request that all buried utilities be marked before you start digging. Plan to give them a few days' lead time to mark buried electrical, cable, and water lines.

Fencing

Fences are something to consider early in the planning stages for most gardeners.

The type of fencing you use will have an impact on the appearance, light exposure, and air movement in your garden. Fencing can even create microclimates. A solid wooden fence at the north end of a garden captures sun from the south, warming the space right in front of it much earlier. Likewise, the ground on the north side of a fence will be shaded and cooler year-round.

Fence material can impact your garden's overall aesthetic and functionality. Choosing something sturdy enough to support vines and possibly espalier trees is another way to increase your garden's productivity and beauty. We use a combination of wire fencing secured by wooden posts with wood privacy fencing throughout our yard and gardens. Three-foot-high chicken wire is enough to deter rabbits from nibbling our berry patches.

Deer fencing for large gardens needs to be at least ten feet high but "micro enclosures" can work, too. This means that fencing in a space eight by sixteen feet or less only needs to be fifty inches high to effectively keep out deer (because they are uncomfortable in small, enclosed spaces).

Vertical Gardening

Growing plants on trellises, arbors, and fences increases your growing capacity while softening your garden borders. We use a variety of trellises, arbors, and cattle panels to get plants up off the ground. Plants like tomatoes, cucumbers, and pole beans are smart choices for vertical gardening. Remember that peas, melons, and even winter squash can all benefit from a lift. And don't forget to add in some flowers like morning glories and nasturtium to your vertical gardening.

CATTLE PANEL TRELLIS

Adding cattle panel trellis arches to your garden space is often a favorite garden project. Not only do they allow you to grow vertically, but they also aesthetically look cool and are relatively inexpensive, especially when you compare it to buying an arch from a garden center ($25ish compared to $200+). You can grow spaghetti squash, vining flowers, runner beans, pumpkins, pickling cucumbers, cucamelons, and even tomatoes on cattle panels.

- Gloves
- Sledgehammer or post driver
- 4 (3') T-posts
- 1 (16' × 50") cattle/hog panel
- Measuring tape
- 12 heavy-duty zip ties (3 per T-post or more if needed)

1. Don your gloves and securely hammer 2 T-posts four feet apart (the width of the cattle/hog panel).
2. The width you make your trellis arch is up to you. Just make sure that the T-posts are an even distance apart and hammered evenly into the ground. Check with a measuring tape.
3. Once the T-posts are secure, with the help of a few people bend the cattle panel into place. Hold the arch in place and once it's bent to your liking, zip tie the metal panel to the T-posts, one at the top of the post, one in the middle, and one toward the bottom.
4. Once all four sides are secured, check for sturdiness of the arch. If you feel that the arch needs more support, add more zip ties.

CATTLE PANEL TOMATO WALL

This makes for a wonderful wall of tomatoes—or any climbing plant, really! You can place two panels next to each other for a roughly eight-foot-wide wall (as directed below) or use in two separate places. You can tie up indeterminate tomatoes on these, with many varieties reaching up and over the wall by the end of the season.

- Gloves
- Bolt cutter
- 1 (16' × 50") cattle/hog panel
- 3 (8'–10') T-posts
- Sledgehammer or post driver
- Measuring tape
- 9 heavy-duty zip ties (3 per T-post or more if needed)

1. Don your gloves and with your bolt cutter cut the cattle/hog panel in half so that you have two 8' × 50" pieces. You can also clip another row of the cross sections at the bottom of the cattle/hog panel to push more into the ground or rely more on the T-posts for stability.
2. Hammer the three T-posts in a line, at least two feet deep, where you want the wall to be, measuring the two outer points and the center point.
3. Place the two sections of cattle/hog panel upright in front of the T-posts and secure with zip ties.

CATTLE PANEL ARCH ON A FENCE

This arch looks great on fences and holds up the heaviest of squash, too! It works best when placed on an existing fence, as it adds the main support. A fun and inexpensive twist on the trendy half-round trellises, having the arch only 20" deep allows for it to "float" and hold up vines.

- Gloves
- Bolt cutter
- 1 (16' × 50") cattle/hog panel
- Roofing screws (or screws with washers)
- Screw gun
- 3 feet (10–16-gauge) wire
- Measuring tape

1. Don your gloves and with your bolt cutter cut the cattle/hog panel in half so that you have two 16' pieces. You'll have one half of the cattle panel that is one "square" bigger than the other, so go back and cut the extra off to make two pieces of the same width, roughly.
2. Then, with at least one more helper place the cattle/hog panel roughly where you want it. Find and mark the top and center of where you want the panel and two equidistant points a little lower and to the sides of the curve. You'll want the screws to be under or "inside" the arch to help hold it in place.
3. With a screw gun, remove the fencing screws nearest the three points marked, twist the wire around the cattle/hog panel and around a roofing screw (or screw with washer) behind the washer. With one helper holding the panel in place, use a screw gun to replace the new screw with wire into the existing fence panel hole. We suggest at least three wire ties/screws per arch.

Garden Styles

Beyond the three traditional garden styles of formal, informal, and wild, vegetable gardens can be broken down into other "types" that fulfill different goals. As you're planning, focus on creating functional, sustainable, and environmentally sound gardens.

IN-GROUND

This is the kind of garden your grandparents likely had. This is what it sounds like; you dig in and plant into the ground. This also includes digging up sod and weeds and amending existing soil.

Pros: A great way to jump into gardening without lots of upfront costs, these kinds of gardens are well suited for growing rows of vegetables, as you'll be walking in and through the garden.

Cons: They require lots of digging which is hard work and can bring up weed seeds. Success depends partially on existing soil. Soil can get compacted and soil drainage can be an issue.

RAISED BED

These gardens have been growing in popularity for good reason: they give you more control with less upkeep once installed. They tend to warm up a little earlier and have excellent drainage.

Pros: Easy to maintain. You control the soil quality, so you tend to get bountiful harvests and less weeding. You can also add mesh to the bottom of beds to keep out burrowing animals, and they can be raised high enough for people with disabilities to work in easily.

Cons: They can call for an expensive initial materials list and more time and skill to install/build.

> ### GARDEN MATH
> How much soil do you need to fill a raised bed? Different soils will settle differently, but a general calculation to use is 1 cubic yard of soil in a 4' × 8' raised bed will fill it about 10" deep. This is the same as 27 cubic feet.

CONTAINER

Container gardening is a terrific solution if you don't have tons of space. You can grow on balconies, roofs, concrete patios, and can spruce up an otherwise bland backdrop such as a front stoop or sidewalk. Container gardening is also useful when growing something outside of your zone. It allows you to bring it indoors during the winter months and back out when the weather is once again adequate for growing. Match the pot to the plant for root needs.

Pros: They can be moved anywhere, and you can completely control the soil.

Cons: The soil dries out faster and cold winters kill many plants in the north.

STRAW BALE

A beneficial way to grow anywhere, using a straw bale as your growing medium does require "conditioning" of the straw with fertilizer and soil to start decomposition. Knowing the source of your straw is important, as some fields are treated with an extremely toxic and persistent herbicide called Grazon. Always ask your supplier before purchasing.

Pros: You can start plants earlier because the decomposition heats up the root zone and creates amazing compost for the following season (you may get two years out of some straw bales).

Cons: Finding a clean source for your straw bales can be difficult and purchasing fertilizer and soil to start the "conditioning" process can add up. It does best with drip irrigation.

EDIBLE LANDSCAPING

Growing food within or as the main part of landscaping is a great way to use your yard efficiently. As with other landscape designs, establishing strong bones is helpful to pull off a visually pleasing edible landscape. As an edible garden changes throughout a growing season, it helps to have something to visually hold it together. Think of switching from spring sugar snap peas to fall broccoli, and that awkward time in between. A trellis, bird bath, large pot, or perennial plants and shrubs can all help accomplish this.

Pros: You can often add vegetables and fruits into existing landscapes, use space already dedicated to gardens, and be able to harvest from existing beds.

Cons: Many common garden plants (beans, greens) have many critters that will eat them (unless fenced off) which can lead to a limited plant selection.

WAYS TO DIG IN—OR NOT

There's a reason you're hearing more about no-dig gardening lately—it really works, and with much less effort than other methods. By placing organic matter on top of the soil you're inviting microorganisms and other decomposers to venture up into that layer and do the "dirty work" for you.

NO-DIG

This process includes "sheet composting," also called "lasagna gardening." You start by adding a layer of cardboard (remove all tape and no glossy cardboard) or many layers of newspaper to recently cut lawn (or weeds). This creates a weed barrier. Then, there are various methods you can follow based on your goals. If you want to plant right away, add at least two inches of finished compost or compost/garden soil mix. By the time the roots reach down to the cardboard layer, it's starting to decompose, and the previous plant life has died back.

If you have a few months before planting, you can add more layers to add depth to your garden bed. I've done this in the fall and planted the following spring in my Minnesota gardens. Add those greens and browns in layers (hence the lasagna reference) with a top dressing of soil to kick-start the process.

Pros: You leave the existing soil structure intact and can build with organic materials that you have on hand. It also harnesses natural processes of decomposition to feed soil (no digging out sod), keeps yard and food waste on site (very economical), and repurposes cardboard.

Cons: Collecting enough of a cardboard/weed barrier can be difficult. It is best to plant in after a few months (unless you build with already finished compost, which costs more).

Hügelkultur is a simple and effective way to boost soil health and grow amazing plants!

HÜGELKULTUR

This combines no-dig with layering and is typically started underground. Place logs and branches at the bottom of a hole, then smaller brush and compostable materials higher up, layering with soil at the top. The idea is that this will take longer to decompose, feeding the soil for longer.

A basic layering recipe could look like: 40 percent logs, 20 percent sticks and branches, 25 percent plant waste (like grass clippings, leaves), 10 percent compost, and 5 percent topsoil. A little more or less of any specific ingredient would work, too

Pros: This system uses materials already on site and sets up the soil to continue decomposing and feeding the soil microorganisms for years. You can use the hügelkultur in metal raised beds as well.

Cons: Digging deep into the ground and not having enough organic material to build it back up.

GARDEN LAYOUT + DESIGN

All that dreaming you've done up to this point will pay off in the long run with happier plants and heartier harvests! We walk through the steps for a vegetable garden below, but the same steps also apply to mapping out your entire yard. Once you start gardening, you'll want to make the most of every square foot so mapping it out on paper will help you see your space in new ways. Keep in mind water, easy access, electrical and zoning requirements for sheds, chicken coops, and so on.

There are as many ways to design and implement a garden as there are gardeners! If there's a friend's or neighbor's garden that you admire, ask them if you can use their plans in your space; garden people love talking about their gardens!

BASIC PLANNING STEPS

1. Draw the garden perimeter.
2. Draw in hardscapes. These non-plant items include fences, paths, and fixed items. This is your "base plan." Make several copies at this point so that you can play with design.
3. Draw a rough outline of garden bed shapes and sizes.
4. Make a list of all the plants you want to grow in your garden (grow what you eat).
5. Draw plants into beds (remembering orientation, spacing, trellising, and harvesting accessibility).
6. Add in companion planting options.
7. Add in succession planting options. (Make spring, summer, and fall versions.)
8. Revise, revise, revise.
9. Save your plans from year to year, make notes, and use for planning crop rotation.

Layout Basics

Garden beds function best when built around three to four feet wide. This allows you to be able to reach the center of any bed without stepping into it.

Main pathways are best kept at two feet wide. Some smaller gardens can get away with eighteen-inch pathways, but if you need to get a wheelbarrow into a space, you'll need a minimum of two feet.

Just a reminder that beds do not have to be straight rows. Depending on materials, the shapes are limited only by your imagination and the space itself.

ORIENTATION

When starting your plant layout, keep in mind the sun's orientation. Plant taller plants on the north end of the bed so that you don't block sun from other shorter plants (unless you want to create shade for lettuces). If you plan on making any of your raised beds into cold frames, know that an east-west orientation with the window slanted toward the south is recommended. See page 41 for cold frame tips.

DESIGN YOUR BASE PLAN

Next is sketching the shape of your garden. Measure existing spaces or walk the area and measure it out. Draw the perimeter of the space to scale on graph paper. Most garden beds will work well when drawn to a scale of one foot to one square on regular graph paper. Then, add existing hardscapes that won't be moving. Stop and make copies of this base plan so that you can make many drafts without having to repeat this step again!

Now's the time to refer to the list of "want to grow" plants you've been gathering. Keep in mind what your family likes to eat most, what you could buy from a local farmer instead, and what is most cost effective to grow. This is the tough part—rarely is their room for all the things we want to grow. Now is the time to compromise.

PLANT SPACING

How you space your plants is going to depend on the kind of gardener you are. Do you like things orderly, or does a little chaos feed your soul? Read the seed packets and consider their recommendations. Many of those packets focus on row gardening, although some are starting to include square foot spacing as well.

Most gardeners (us included!) struggle with remembering just how big plants really get by the end of the growing season. Giving plants ample space will help them flourish and make your late season gardening jobs more enjoyable, too. Spacing plants too close can decrease air flow and light, both of which can lead to weakened plants. Weak plants are more susceptible to disease and pest pressure. I tend to crowd my plants a little but am aware that I then need to pay extra attention to them. Also, the more crowded the plants, the trickier the harvest.

The chart on the following page is a guideline for both spacing and a suggested number of plants per family of four. Combine how you'll be planting (either row or square foot) with how many plants you want to grow to give yourself an idea of how much space you'll need to grow what you want.

START PLACING PLANTS

Taking into consideration the elements we went over before, start placing plants into your base plan. You'll likely move things around quite a few times as you work this out.

This is the step where some garden alchemy happens—you're using your imagination along with your experience. This process gets easier to see each time you do it. Think about all season long. Imagine pollinators, harvesting, and how the sun changes. Getting a plan on paper will help you visualize the garden better but, remember, there's nothing like seeing a garden grow throughout the seasons. Living the experience is really what it's all about anyway—and nature is the best teacher.

Try keeping a record of what you grew in which garden spaces. I tend to lean on my Instagram account and story archives for this, along with a spreadsheet of seed-starting dates and a few notes on how plants performed. This practice helps you fine-tune your garden skills year after year. It also helps you practice crop rotation in the future.

Plant Spacing Chart

	Between Plants in Rows	Between Rows	Square Foot Planting / square foot	Plants per family of 4
Asparagus	10–16"	12–18"	1	16–20
Bush Beans	2–4"	12"	10	50–60
Pole Beans	4–6"	Trellis	4	30–40
Beets	3–5"	8"	9	50–60 (½ spring, ½ fall)
Broccoli	18–24"	24"	1	25–30
Brussels Sprouts	24"	18–36"	<1	6–8
Cabbage, savoy	12–18"	18–36"	1	15–20 (½ spring, ½ fall)
Cabbage, storage	12–18"	18–36"	1	10–15
Carrots	1–2"	10"	16	300–400
Cauliflower	18–24"	24"	1	25–35
Celery	12"	18"	2	10–15
Chard	6–9"	12–18"	2	4–8
Cucumber	8–12"	Trellis	2	4–8
Garlic	4–6"	4–6"	9	40–80
Kale	12–18"	18"	1	4–8
Kohlrabi	4"	12"	4	20–30 (½ spring, ½ fall)
Lettuce	6–12"	12"	6	30–50 (½ spring, ½ fall)
Leeks	3–5"	8"	9	15–20
Melons	36–48"	36–48"	<1	2–4
Onions	4–5"	12"	9	70–100
Pak Choi	10–14"	18"	4	12–20
Peas, Snap	2"	Trellis	9	60–80 (½ spring, ½ fall)
Peppers	18"	24–30"	1	10–15
Potatoes	9–12"	24–30"	2	50–75
Radish	1–2"	2–4"	16	50–75 (½ spring, ½ fall)
Spinach	3–5"	8"	9	40–60 (½ spring, ½ fall)
Squash (summer)	36–48"	36–48"	<1	3–5
Squash (winter)	36–48"	48–60"	<1	2–4
Tomatoes, Cherry	20–30"	30" (trellis)	<1	2–3
Tomatoes, slicer/canner	20–30"	30" (trellis)	<1	20–24

TENDING THE HOMESTEAD GARDEN

There is a deep joy that takes root in us as we tend our gardens through the seasons. Nurturing seedlings into blooming gardens that become habitat for wildlife and food for pollinators and our families, all while building the soil, forms a bond between us and nature that becomes stronger each season.

Let's look at eco-friendly ways of tending our gardens while making the most of our space and time. And I'll confess that the job of weeding can either be treasured meditation time . . . or the task I most dread. Garden maintenance is a great time to call on your community; weeding always goes faster with family and friends. Having another set of eyes to figure out what disease or pest is attacking your plants helps, too!

Composting

Composting is truly one of the best things you can do for your garden, and the planet.

If you care about growing your own food, chances are you also care about food waste. "America generated more than 63 million tons of food waste in 2018" according to the EPA's latest numbers. That's over a pound a day of wasted food, and about 40 percent of the total food grown for human consumption in the United States. Barely 4 percent of that total is composted. The amount of energy loss represented in this number is staggering.

Let those numbers sink in. Still, compost is garden gold for our gardens, helping keep moisture and more available nutrients in the soil. And the biggest bonus of compost is how it creates a carbon-rich environment to welcome microbes to make those nutrients more available

We ended up with a makeshift three-phase compost setup. It helps us keep composting throughout the seasons as we move more finished compost to a new bin (kind of like succession planting our compost!).

to the plants. This builds a more resilient soil food web, which grows better crops for you. Mother Nature for the win!

COMPOST SETUP

There are countless ways to compost, from "cold" piles that take a year or two to fully decompose, to hot piles done in a few weeks, underground systems, bokashi systems (which actually ferment organic matter with a specific bacterium, not decompose it), vermicomposting (worm farms), and everything in between. We'll focus on the typical aboveground compost pile and provide you with the knowledge to control the outcome!

Even though I refer to this as garden gold, it is not a jewel in the landscape. So, an out of the way corner, preferably partially shaded, makes a great home for your compost piles. There are many premade compost bins and tumblers available and if that gets you started, then great! We like our wood slat or wire fencing versions because they sit on the ground and keep it cooking longer into our cold winters.

Plan for at least 3' × 3' space so that the pile has enough mass to heat up properly. Larger than 4' × 4' and it gets tough to turn the piles. We've got wood, wire fencing, and an old potato growing tube being used as composting sites. Just make sure there's open space for air flow, and that you can remove, open, or dig into it for turning and harvesting.

Research shows that compost piles should heat up to roughly 140°F for two weeks to completely kill the seeds, spores, and eggs of the things you don't want to grow in your garden. The heat comes from the microorganisms giving off gas as they eat and decompose the pile.

LEAF MOLD IS MAGIC, TOO!

Leaf mold is simply a pile of leaves left to sit for one to three years. These decompose into a carbon-rich soil amendment that holds onto water, feeds the soil, and keeps the soil structure loose. While leaf mold doesn't contain any available nutrients, it makes a great mulch! **Don't add walnut tree leaves, as they emit juglone, a toxin for plants, and oak tree leaves add high tannin levels to the soil so keep to under 50 percent.**

RECIPE FOR COMPOST SUCCESS

Decomposition thrives on carbon- and nitrogen-rich organic materials. In composting lingo, carbon-rich items are called "browns." I think of them as the bulking ingredient. Nitrogen-rich items are called "greens." I think of these as the energy ingredient.

Start with roughly two to three parts browns (dried leaves, dried grass clippings, straw, wood chips, newspaper, cardboard) and one part greens (food scraps, fresh grass clippings, coffee grounds, fresh manure, garden waste), plus enough water to keep it damp. **Avoid composting diseased plants.** Alternate browns and greens in layers as best you can. This recipe, plus turning your compost pile every week to introduce lots of oxygen into the system, should result in finished compost in four to six months. Check on your pile often, keeping it from drying out or becoming waterlogged.

If you're able to monitor it closely, turn the pile if it reaches 160°F, as getting too hot can kill off the good organisms doing the decomposing.

GARDEN-READY

You'll know your compost is ready to use when it looks and smells like rich soil. The top may not be quite as ready as the bottom half, even if you've been turning it. I tend to turn my compost as I harvest it by moving the top half to a new pile.

I also like using partially composted materials when I'm building new garden beds to give the "composting in place" a jump start.

Not into making your own compost? Collect your yard waste and food scraps and bring to a local county facility where they compost for you! There are many local sites throughout the states and across the globe—just do an online search for "composting sites near me."

Soil Health

Soil is the "ground zero" starting point for the health of your garden and the food you grow. Understanding a little about how soil and plants work together can help you grow nutrient-dense crops. Soil is a living, breathing thing full of microorganisms like fungi, invertebrates, worms, bacteria, algae, nematodes, and protozoa to name a few. When we till or use pesticides or herbicides, we destroy the existing microorganisms in the soil food web. Using fewer chemicals and moving toward organic gardening is my hope for all of us homesteaders!

Did you know an average teaspoon of healthy soil contains between one hundred million and one billion living microorganisms? Just take a minute to let that settle. Up to one billion. Not a typo. This shows us a glimpse of the intricate beauty of nature.

Scientists are constantly learning more about the soil food web that drives the availability of nutrients to plants. These relationships do best when left undisturbed, which is why no-dig gardening is becoming so popular.

Soil is a limited resource, as it can take several hundred years for one inch to form. Most soil around suburban homes has been disturbed but is still alive. As gardeners, we can nurture this resource to help us grow our food!

SOIL STYLE

How do you know what kind of soil you have?

First, just dig in. How does it feel? Did you find any earthworms? Does it crumble or squish? Is it loamy or sandy? Does it stay wet after a rain or dry out quickly? Do plants grow well there? You can tell a lot about soil health by taking a closer look.

Interested in learning more about your soil? Get it tested! Soil tests are available through most state university extension offices and countless private labs worldwide. Most of these services provide a few different levels of testing and recommendations. Our local university performs basic soil tests for under $20. Some labs also offer home compost analysis.

MICHELLE'S SOIL TEST EXPERIENCE

I decided to have both my front yard and vegetable garden soil tested a few years ago. At the time of the testing, my front yard had remained static for twenty-plus years. The back

Soil Test Results

Sample/Field Number: VEGG

SOIL TEST RESULTS

Estimated Soil Texture	Organic Matter %	Soluble Salts mmhos/cm	pH	Buffer Index	Nitrate NO3-N ppm	Olsen Phosphorus ppm P	Bray 1 Phosphorus ppm P	Potassium ppm K	Sulfur SO4 -S ppm	Zinc ppm	Iron ppm	Manganese ppm	Copper ppm	Boron ppm	Calcium ppm	Magnesium ppm	Lead ppm
Coarse	9.8		7.1				88	91									

INTERPRETATION OF SOIL TEST RESULTS

Phosphorus (P) PPPPPPPPPPPPPPPPPPPPPPPPPPPPPPPPPPPPPPPPP
5 — Low   10   15 — Medium   20   25 — High   V. High

Potassium (K) KKKKKKKKKKK
25 — Low   75   125 — Medium   175 — High   225   V. High

pH **
3.0   4.0   5.0   6.0   7.0   8.0   9.0
Acid   Optimum   Alkaline

Soluble Salts
0 1.0 2.0 3.0 4.0 5.0 6.0 7.0 8.0 9.0 10.0
Satisfactory   Possible Problem   Excessive Salts

RECOMMENDATIONS FOR: Vegetable garden

Sample/Field Number: FRONT

SOIL TEST RESULTS

Estimated Soil Texture	Organic Matter %	Soluble Salts mmhos/cm	pH	Buffer Index	Nitrate NO3-N ppm	Olsen Phosphorus ppm P	Bray 1 Phosphorus ppm P	Potassium ppm K	Sulfur SO4 -S ppm	Zinc ppm	Iron ppm	Manganese ppm	Copper ppm	Boron ppm	Calcium ppm	Magnesium ppm	Lead ppm
Coarse	2.8		6.0				37	207									

INTERPRETATION OF SOIL TEST RESULTS

Phosphorus (P) PPPPPPPPPPPPPPPPPPPPPPPPPPPPPPPPPPPPPPPPPPPPP
5 — Low   10   15 — Medium   20   25 — High   V. High

Potassium (K) KKKKKKKKKKKKKKKKKKKKKKKKKKKKK
25 — Low   75   125 — Medium   175 — High   225   V. High

pH *********************************
3.0   4.0   5.0   6.0   7.0   8.0   9.0
Acid   Optimum   Alkaline

Soluble Salts
0 1.0 2.0 3.0 4.0 5.0 6.0 7.0 8.0 9.0 10.0
Satisfactory   Possible Problem   Excessive Salts

RECOMMENDATIONS FOR: Small fruits

The biggest difference was the percentage of organic matter. Only 2.8 percent in the front yard, compared to 9.8 percent in the vegetable garden!

vegetable garden had compost and organic matter added to it for two years. The numbers speak for themselves!

I was happy to see my hard work of composting in place and hauling compost to the garden paying off. The slightly acidic soil in the front yard is also why blueberries do well there.

SOIL TESTING

Soil tests tend to look at the levels of a few specific elements in the soil. These results don't take into account the vast soil food web relationships, but they give us a really good place to start.

Dig down into the root zone of the soil. Take four to six samples from different areas you want to test. Mix the soil together in the bucket. You'll be submitting between one and three cups of soil in total, depending on the specific lab instructions. Remember to test garden and lawn soils separately.

Results will include pH levels which are important for the uptake of nutrients in the soil. A lower pH level means the soil is more acidic (good for blueberries and those blue hydrangea), and higher pH means the soil is more alkaline (also called "sweet" soil). A pH level of 6.5 is considered ideal for most vegetables, but anywhere between 6 and 7 is going to grow good veggies.

Soil acidity levels have noticeable impacts on which nutrients are available in the soil. This highlights another one of those amazing relationships in our soil; even though you have lots of phosphorus in your soil, if your pH is below 6.5 your plants could have trouble absorbing it.

The soil elements that are most important to growing plants and most often tested for are N-P-K; nitrogen, phosphorus, and potassium/potash:

Nitrogen can be added to the garden with composted manure, blood or feather meal, fish emulsion, or coffee grounds.

Phosphorus can be added with bone meal, rock phosphate, or composted manure. Many states currently ban phosphorus fertilizer use or sale, as the overuse of this nutrient leads to poor water quality, so use only if suggested.

Potassium/potash can be added with kelp meal and wood ash (ash raises pH levels).

BEST PRACTICES IN THE GARDEN

MULCH
If there is a secret weapon in maintaining my vegetable gardens and the soil, it's mulch! Mulch keeps the weeds down, prevents soil-borne diseases from spreading, adds carbon to my soil, and conserves water.

What make a good mulch? Things like straw, pine shavings, dried grass clippings, or leaves. Wood chips and pine bark are mulches best left on top of the soil.

In the fall, once the wettest season has passed, I'll often add a layer of compost to the gardens as a mulch. Technically, finished compost is considered a mulch. Since it doesn't seem to do much to fend off soil-borne diseases splashing up on leaves, I tend to only use it as a mulch later in the season.

CROP ROTATION
Practicing crop rotation keeps your garden healthy. It is most valuable with tomatoes, potatoes, squash, and cucumbers (Solanaceae and Cucurbitaceae families), as these plants tend to attract the most pests that overwinter in the soil. By moving the crops from one garden bed to another, you make it harder for the insects and diseases to find what they need to eat. This is an effective tactic that helps organic gardeners maintain healthy gardens—but not something to stress out about, especially if you didn't see any signs of disease or pests the year before.

WATERING
In general, most vegetable plants need roughly one inch of water per week during the growing season. Remember to water at the soil level, not on a plant's leaves. Watering more deeply but less often will encourage better root growth. Watering in the morning is typically the best option, as any splashed water will dry off in the sun, and lower temperatures mean more water will soak into the ground rather than evaporate.

RAIN BARRELS
Rain barrels are a great way to collect water destined to run off your property. Rain barrel water is usually slightly acidic which is excellent for nutrient uptake by plants. Harvested rainwater should be applied to the soil level. As

an extra safety precaution, you can wait to harvest a full day after watering to benefit from the sun's ultraviolet light disinfection of any possible contaminants. If an option, try using rainwater on nonedible plants to avoid contamination. If you are interested in more information, visit the EPA's website at https://www.epa.gov/.

WEEDING

Regardless of how well we plan our gardens, there will be weeds. Some of my favorite foraged foods are considered weeds: stinging nettles for tea, purslane and lamb's quarters for salads, and dandelions for jelly. Weeds are actually wonderful at bringing nutrients into our soil. But in general, we want to keep the weeds controlled in our vegetable gardens, as weeds compete for available resources with the plants we're intentionally growing. They're also persistent and tend to grow more quickly than most cultivated plants.

Knowing more about the weed in question will help you get rid of them with less effort. My best advice (why don't I follow it better?) is to get them when they're small! Also know that no garden is weed-free!

FERTILIZING

Did you know we're more likely to overfertilize our gardens than even our lawns? Referring to your soil test can help you decide what, if any, amendments need to be made to your garden soil in general.

I do fertilize as I'm transplanting seedlings into the garden. I mix an organic slow-release fertilizer into the holes as I'm planting out seedlings. I'll fertilize tomatoes and peppers once more later in the summer. If you know your garden soil is lacking in nutrients, you can feed up to every four weeks. The following slow-release fertilizer mix has worked well for me over the years:

SLOW-RELEASE FERTILIZER MIX

- 3 parts soybean or some kind of seed meal
- 1 part agricultural lime or gypsum
- 1 part bone meal
- ½ part kelp meal

1. Check your local feed mill for soybean meal, which is often sold in fifty-pound bags, so this recipe can make a lot! You can ask to break a bag in half for you or find a garden friend and split a batch.
2. Mix together ingredients outdoors or in a well-ventilated space.

You can also skip mixing your own and buy smaller amounts of complete 3–3–3 or 4–4–4 organic fertilizer to use instead. The main idea is to add a boost to the soil at transplant time that will minimize transplant shock and help the plant thrive all season long.

PRUNING

Pruning dead or diseased parts of plants will help keep your garden healthier. I also prune tomato plant leaves up to a foot or more above the soil to avoid transferring soil-borne diseases to low leaves. Keeping good air flow in between your vegetable plants will help the plants and make harvesting easier, too.

Make sure to clean your pruning shears after each cut on a diseased plant and in between other jobs. A simple hand sanitizer spray or bleach solution works. Remember to discard diseased plant material in the garbage, burn it, or bring it to a high heat composting facility. Do not add it to your own compost pile, as it will likely not get hot enough for long enough to kill the disease.

Succession Planting

Succession planting helps spread out your harvests and keeps foods ripening for longer. By staggering your seed-starting dates, planting times, varieties, and crops throughout the season you can harvest more consistently from your garden.

SUCCESSION PLANTING STRATEGIES

Succession planting can mean a lot of different things to different gardeners. It boils down to keeping the garden bed full, with more crops following each other in the same space. The key

for me is starting early and being mindful of the varieties I grow.

- Fast food crops like leaf lettuces and radishes that mature in thirty to fifty days can be replanted every few weeks to keep fresh harvests rolling in, often called relay planting. Or you could plant those fast crops early as placeholders for other heat-loving crops that will be planted later.
- Keep starting seeds throughout the season. We often think of starting seeds inside during the late winter/early spring to then plant out for the summer, but by starting a few crops (like carrots, cabbages, and broccoli) mid-season, you can easily harvest a fall succession from the same space.
- Interplanting combines succession and companion planting practices. For example, plant fast-maturing lettuce and radishes in between peppers as an understory; they'll receive less light and be harvested before the peppers grow into the space.

I start the earliest seeds like onions and peppers mid-February and keep on seeding new crops like lettuce and radishes through mid-August. This can seem like a daunting task so, as in all things, start small, and build your knowledge and comfort with it each season. I'm still learning with each season, too!

A great place to start is by sowing a second set of fall brassicas, such as broccoli or cauliflower, ten to twelve weeks before the first expected frost in fall (mid-June for us northern gardeners) and see how that feels. Having a plan for where those will go can be as easy as replacing your spring crop of broccoli and cauliflower.

Early spring has us longing for fresh greens, and that is exactly what grows well in the cool spring weather. We can reap another fall harvest of heartier greens if we start more seeds in early July (for my zone 4). By practicing a few of these techniques in tandem with some season extension (see page 37), you can harvest more food for longer each year.

DEALING WITH PESTS + DISEASES

Integrated Pest Management (IPM)

Integrated Pest Management, known as IPM, offers a thoughtful framework for looking at all kinds of issues in the garden. This model asserts the least invasive options be applied first, giving nature a chance to shine through.

Common Garden Pests

There are literally thousands of different garden pests throughout the world—so this book isn't going to even attempt to name them all. What we can say is spending time in your garden with an insect identification book will give you quite an education.

UNIVERSITY OF MINNESOTA
EXTENSION

INTEGRATED PEST MANAGEMENT (IPM) BASICS
MASTER GARDENER VOLUNTEER PROGRAM

ABOUT THIS GUIDE

Integrated Pest Management is an effective and environmentally conscious way to deal with pest problems in the garden. Use this guide to direct your approach when managing pests. Remember to use science-based information to inform your decisions.

STEP 1:
BUILD KNOWLEDGE

STEP 2:
DECISION MAKING

STEP 3:
CONTROL TACTICS

Learn about your pest problem. Ask yourself:

- What is the **life cycle** of the pest?
- How does this pest **behave**?
- What are the **population dynamics**?
- How does this pest interact with the **environment**?
- What is the host plant **life cycle**?

REMEMBER: Pests can include insects, diseases, weeds, and even animals.

Decide how to best take action by asking:

- How serious is the damage?
- Is the problem getting worse?
- Will the plant recover?
- Is it worth treating?
- **Do I want to take action?**

REMEMBER: Sometimes not taking any action is the best decision (e.g., learning to adapt to the problem, or choosing to grow other plants to avoid the problem).

IF TAKING ACTION → Go to **STEP 3** to implement control tactic(s).

Implement control tactics to effectively manage pest problems.

The methods listed below follow a continuum. Start with preventative cultural methods, and if problems emerge, try physical control strategies. If needed, chemical and biological control options can be explored.

CULTURAL
▽
PHYSICAL
▽
BIOLOGICAL
▽
CHEMICAL

ASSESS how the control tactics are working. You many need to revisit **STEP 1** and/or **STEP 2** to refine your management strategy if your approach is not working.

© C. Marsden (author) & N. Hoidal (contributor), University of Minnesota, 2018.

When doing an online search for information on a pest or disease in your garden, try adding ".edu or extension" and look for information near your area to find researched information.

A great place to start digging deeper into the world of garden pests is Jessica Walliser's book, *Good Bug, Bad Bug*.

If you find an infestation of insects, take a minute to learn just a little more about them. Is this their larval stage, what do they turn into, where do they go at night, how do they reproduce, what do they eat? Asking these questions can really help you plan your attack. In most organic gardens, the first plan of attack is hand picking. Some usual suspects include:

- Imported cabbage worms
- Cabbage loopers
- Cucumber beetles
- Cut worms
- Potato bug
- Japanese beetles
- Jumping worms
- Tomato hornworms
- Slugs
- Squash vine borers

(By the way, all of these bugs are chicken-approved treats!)

Imported cabbageworm.

Keeping Critters Out

An easy way to deter animals like rabbits and squirrels from hanging out in your garden is to remove habitat like brush piles, nesting area, and food sources. The stinky repellants (blood meal, etc.) are especially effective for rabbits, but rabbits also tend to get comfortable with whatever you use, so the name of the game here is to change it up often. You also might want to find out what your neighbors have been using to keep rabbits out of their gardens and use something different! Also, be aware of what nutrients you're adding to your soil when spreading these deterrents.

ROW COVER

Lightweight row covers can really help keep pests off your plants. Be aware that the edges must be tucked in tight to avoid tiny insects from entering. Frequent checking under the cover is also important so that you don't miss an infestation caught with rather than kept from your crop.

ORGANIC PEST SPRAY

Sometimes the bugs become too much, and you need a solution. This simple pest spray works great on any soft-bodied larvae like cabbage worms and potato bugs, as well as aphids, leafhoppers, thrips, and mealy bugs. Spray in the morning or evening and avoid using in full sun. As with all natural remedies, this will have to be reapplied more often.

In a 1-quart spray bottle, mix in ¼ cup olive oil, 1 tablespoon castile soap, and fill the rest of the bottle with water. Swirl (don't shake, to avoid suds) before each use. Spray directly on soft-bodied pests. Repeat every day or two as new pests emerge. This mixture has a short shelf life of a few weeks.

DISEASES

Biodiverse gardens will generally have less disease pressure than monocrops. Diseases can come from the soil or be spread by pests as they chew into plant matter or leave their droppings. Fusarium wilt is a bacterial disease brought by insects.

Powdery mildew is a common fungal disease spread by spores. Thankfully, powdery mildew doesn't usually reduce the harvest. Tomato blights, both early and late, can severely decrease harvests and overwinters in soil and plant material. Again, remember: Good garden planning and being present in your garden can help you catch issues in time to deal with them!

Harvesting

Try to harvest in the morning once dew is dried, not in the heat of the afternoon. Keep produce out of direct light and cooled off as soon as possible. Giving a good rinse to food that is dirty is generally a good idea, but it's advisable to wait on washing most crops, as getting them wet shortens their storage life (because washing begins the process of degradation).

BROCCOLI HARVESTING TIP

Soak your harvested broccoli and cauliflower in cold salt water (a teaspoon or two per big bowl) for ten minutes before cooking to reveal any hiding creepy crawlies. They'll float to the top within a few minutes, saving you the worry.

PERPETUAL GROWTH

I take loads of pictures (see my Instagram feed @forksinthedirt for ample proof) to remember exactly how these plants grew together, how they did in this spot versus that, and other notes. This will help you maintain an even better garden the following year and give your spirit a boost during those non-gardening times of the year.

COMPANION PLANTING

Companion Planting Techniques

Gardens that incorporate companion planting techniques are more colorful, bountiful, and resilient with biodiversity. It is this abundance of life that mimics nature and provides the garden (and gardener) with a host of mutually beneficial relationships. It is in these relationships where we see lasting benefits:

- Growing a wider variety of crops in general.
- Adding more flowers to the vegetable garden.
- Growing crops to build the soil.
- Growing crops to inhibit diseases.
- Growing crops to welcome beneficial insects.
- Growing crops to deter pests.
- Planting specific crops next to each other.

While there are many specific relationships under the companion planting umbrella, it is the synergy and diversity of plants that make this an idea worth putting into practice. The more biodiverse our gardens, the more flexible and stable they are as well.

Companion planting has drawn on folklore for generations. A new generation of gardeners and scientists are now testing out these long-held beliefs. Planting certain plant families and varieties together can help them feed each other and conserve resources, as shallow and deep-rooted plants thrive side by side. It just makes sense to use nature's existing plant powers in our gardens.

BUILDING SOIL WITH COMPANION PLANTING

Keeping our garden soil covered helps feed the microorganisms, avoid compaction, and decrease evaporation, all ways to build healthy soil. And, yes, we talk about soil in a few different ways throughout the book because it really is *that* important!

KEEP IT COVERED

A great way to build your soil is by planting cover crops. I prefer cover crops that die back over winter, called "winter kill" crops. My favorite general purpose seed mix consists of oats, peas, and radishes. This blend gives an all-around nitrogen boost to the soil and creates biomass both above and below the soil surface.

It also loosens the soil structure below ground while feeding soil microorganisms by leaving the plants to die back in place. Seeds generally only need five to six weeks of growing time to be effective. Make sure to chop down or let nature freeze the plants before seeds mature unless you want that crop to continue.

If cover cropping seems like too much work, use mulch instead. In the fall, a great way to use all those tree leaves is to place them right onto your beds and skip the bagging! Both mulching and cover cropping can build soil by introducing more organic matter.

DECREASING DISEASE PRESSURE

Much of a vegetable garden's disease pressure comes from soil-borne diseases. Practicing good plant spacing and crop rotation will lower the ability of many of these diseases to thrive. Crop rotation moves plant families to different parts of the garden every year, typically in a four-year cycle. This is most important for tomatoes, potatoes, and peppers, as they have the most disease and pest pressure.

Another proven companion planting strategy is to interplant an understory of shorter, denser plants like lettuces, carrots, sweet alyssum, thyme, etc. to decrease the splash-up on the bottom leaves of plants. Having infected soil splash up onto leaves is a common way for those plants to become infected. Interplanting can include planting fast-maturing plants between slower-maturing plants and shade-loving plants under taller plants. I love how this way of planting can

An example of interplanting and companion planting in a spring garden bed. Peas at the back are fixing nitrogen for heavy-feeding broccoli. Fast-growing kohlrabi will be harvested soon, giving more space for broccoli to continue growing. Lettuces are growing underneath, calendula are a nearby flower bringing in beneficial insects, while a ground cover of thyme surrounds the bed, acting as an egg-laying deterrent for cabbage moths.

literally double the harvests out of the same area of garden.

PLANT USES

Plants release chemicals in response to environmental changes. They can respond to insect attacks by releasing these different chemical scents into the air (different from their fragrances, though). When a "distress" chemical is released, it can warn other nearby plants, and/or call on other beneficial insects to feast on the pest attacking it. Talk about plant power!

Certain plants can be used in the garden as a trap crop, which means they are planted as

Michelle's vegetable garden pollinator runway.

sacrificial offerings to pest insects to lure them away from your prized vegetable plants.

Examples: Radishes planted alongside cabbages to lure flea beetles into eating those radish leaves instead of your cabbages, or a Hubbard squash planted in your pumpkin patch to lure squash vine borers away from other squash. Gardeners can also use a flower's natural scent as a masking plant. The best-known example is the marigold.

Varying plant and leaf shapes can be used to confuse egg-laying habits of pest insects, effectively stopping the next generation of pests from hatching. Research shows that planting dill in between cabbages can confuse cabbage loopers enough that they will keep hunting for another place to lay their eggs.

Welcoming Beneficial Insects

Attracting beneficial insects will help pollinate your crops and control the pest insects. Beneficial insects are those that are predatory or parasitic to pest insects and/or help pollinate your intended plants. The best way to attract these insects is to create an environment that welcomes them in year after year. This means giving them food, water, and shelter.

PERENNIAL POLLINATOR PLANTS

I tend perennial flower gardens around my yard and close to my vegetable gardens. I've dubbed the path to my vegetable garden the "pollinator runway," and it literally buzzes with dozens of varieties of pollinators from spring to fall.

Plant a large and dense enough area to be effective, a 4' × 4' square is a great start. Pollinators and plants evolved together, so

Meadow blazing star (Liatris ligulistylis).

choosing plants native to your area helps you attract your native pollinators. Most pollinating insects prefer to have sources of both pollen and nectar close at hand. Choosing pollinator plants can provide complete food sources along with habitat for egg laying, pupation, and hibernation. By providing bloom from the earliest to the latest possible dates for your zone, you welcome season-long pollination and protection.

What makes a good pollinator plant? A combination of a rich nectar source, lots of pollen, bright colors, and fragrant blooms!

FAVORITE PERENNIAL POLLINATOR PLANTS (FOR ZONE 4)

* Milkweed (*Asclepias syriaca*)
* Meadow blazing star (*Liatris ligulistylis*)
* Giant blue hyssop (*Agastache foeniculum*)
* Bee balm (*Monarda fistulosa*)
* Yarrow (*Achillea millefolium*)
* Aster (*Symphyotrichum oolentangiense*)
* Coneflower (*Echinacea*)
* False indigo (*Baptisia*)
* Comfrey (*Symphytum*) *non-native

Flowers in the daisy family, known as composite flowers, are a fabulous flower type used in most gardens to fulfill most of these needs. Almost all my favorites are composites, as they provide so much to the visiting bees, butterflies, moths, hoverflies, and other pollinators that bring our gardens to life.

Annual Companion Flowers

Annuals can be started indoors or direct sown each year to bring beauty, nectar, pollen, and other powers to your vegetable gardens! These are mostly easy to start and save from seed and can be started indoors or direct sown.

Bouquet includes calendula, cosmos, marigold, and nasturtium—all companion flower powerhouses.

CALENDULA

Calendula produces a sticky resin that attracts both pests and the good guys such as ladybugs, lacewings, and hoverflies which control destructive pests. I always try to grow enough to make some of my soothing calendula salve, too (see recipe on page 121).

COSMOS

This plant attracts the bright green long-legged fly, hoverflies, bees, parasitic wasps, butterflies, and even birds. Those beneficial bugs and birds nibble pests like aphids, squash beetles, etc.

MARIGOLDS

Previously, botanists believed that this plant's strong odor deterred insects from coming around, but research has shown that marigolds actually mask other plants' smells. They produce a substance called alpha-terthienyl, a chemical that also suppresses pest nematodes and cabbage worms.

SUNFLOWERS

These tallest of the annual flowers bring literal sunshine into the garden along with beneficial insects, and birds—which eat pests at an even faster rate. They can also be used as a trellis to grow cucumbers and other vining vegetables. **Read seed packet descriptions closely! Some new hybrid sunflowers for the cut flower market are pollenless and still contain some nectar but will not produce seed.** Consider wrapping heads of sunflowers in netting if you want to harvest seeds for yourself. Seeds are easy to store for next year and make a fun snack when boiled and roasted.

MEXICAN SUNFLOWERS (*TITHONIA*)

These pollinator powerhouses grow their own multi-stemmed flower jungle from one seed. With a branching habit and blooms that keep going until frost, these are the most visited annual flowers by the monarch super generation.

ZINNIAS

Zinnias deter cucumber beetles and tomato hornworms. They attract predatory wasps and hoverflies, which eat insects that would otherwise destroy garden plants. Zinnias attract hummingbirds, which eat whiteflies before those flies can damage tomatoes, cucumbers, and potatoes.

SWEET ALYSSUM

Sweet Alyssum are not a composite flower, but so valuable that they made the list. This sweet-smelling, low-growing annual flower also deters root maggots, helping keep your carrots and potatoes healthy. Purchase seeds.

NASTURTIUM

Nasturtiums' color pops, and their ability to climb and/or drape in the garden, along with being completely edible (hello, spicy!), make them a fun addition to the vegetable garden. They also attract hoverflies, which munch on aphids and have been shown to deter squash bugs. They're easy to save and start from seed as well. They need darkness to germinate.

Plant Combinations

While there really is so much more to companion planting than "grow this next to that" there are some researched, mutually beneficial plant relationships. One of the oldest and most well-known is the Native American planting of the Three Sisters Garden. This plan interplants corn, beans, and squash. The corn creates a pole for the beans to climb but requires lots of nitrogen to produce well. The beans are natural nitrogen fixers, pulling nitrogen out of the air and bringing it into the soil, so, the beans nourish the corn even as they grow up its stalks. The squash, with its low-growing habit, shades the soil, helping conserve water and keeping down weed growth.

Three sisters growing tip: Wait until your corn plants are a few inches tall before planting your beans. This will ensure that the corn is strong enough to support the vining beans all season long.

The results of these mutually beneficial relationships can often be seen aboveground

This is an example of companion planting using beans as a nitrogen fixer while growing up the trellis with tomatoes. Celery and basil are alternated in front of the tomatoes, adding both pest deterrence and flavor enhancement. Carrots are a great layer between these crops, with differing root depths and nutrient needs. Adding a front row of sweet alyssum brings in beneficial insects.

and at harvest time. Being aware of what is working or not is a key to figuring out what plants grow well together in your specific garden environment. Learning as you go about the depth of roots, water, and nutrient needs of plants will have you placing plants that will do well next to each other in a few short seasons.

HERBS AS COMPANION PLANTS

Herbs are a powerful addition to the companion plant list. Many herbs have strong masking and trap cropping traits, but each relationship below works for different reasons. Borage gets a special mention because, though self-seeding, it plays well with all the common vegetable plants!

HAPPY HERB + VEGETABLE PLANT COMBINATIONS

- Basil + tomato
- Chives + carrots
- Dill/Mint + brassicas
- Sage + melons
- Thyme + brassicas

PLANT COMBINATIONS TO AVOID

- Tomatoes + potatoes/cabbages
- Potatoes + cucumbers/melons
- Beans/peas + alliums
- Peppers + beans
- Fennel appreciates its own space

EXTENDING THE GROWING SEASON

Let's get you growing more food in the same space by extending each season. It's truly so empowering to use one or more of the season extension methods to extend the time a plant can grow or stay living in the soil. By combining a few of the following season extension methods, you can easily add weeks and possibly months to your growing season. That extra time can enable even northern gardeners to get at least two (sometimes three!) successions of many crops.

One key is starting with the best variety for your purpose. For northern gardeners like me, this means finding the cold-hardy, fast-maturing plant varieties to start our spring off with a bang. Extending the growing season is all about harnessing nature's power and tendencies from

Low tunnel at work.

existing plant traits to microclimates. Luckily, farmers and gardeners have been doing this for centuries, so we have lots of accumulated knowledge to draw from. This information is based on our zone 4b homestead, but applicable to all but the warmest growing zones. Find your growing zone on page 131.

For most of us, season extension will involve using a combination of methods including:

- Starting seeds indoors
- Growing in low tunnels
- Growing in cold frames
- Using cloches
- Winter sowing

BEGIN WITH OBSERVATION

Notice what plants start growing earliest in your yard, and where. Think of the early season perennials like chives, asparagus, and rhubarb. By placing those specific plants in your yard's warmest microclimates, you can start eating a few weeks earlier simply through thoughtful plant placement. Pay attention to south-facing hills, natural wind barriers, and even soil color which can all bring earlier spring harvests.

For me, eating from the garden earlier is worth the effort. The process sometimes involves shoveling snow off my cold frame, checking my newly transplanted babies in the low tunnel during that late season snowstorm, and opening to vent on sunny days but, as with all projects on your homestead, work on finding that sweet spot for you. Take a season or two and play with how much time, energy, and money you are willing to put into harvesting out of your garden earlier.

AIR TEMPERATURE VS. SOIL TEMPERATURE

Luckily for seedlings and plant roots, soil temperatures are much more consistent compared to fluctuating air temperatures. It is soil temperatures that you need to pay attention to for germinating the earliest plants. As the seed starting chart on page 46 shows, many plants will germinate at low soil temperatures. Having a dedicated thermometer to track soil temps will help you keep a handle on things. I have both an old meat thermometer and a soil thermometer that help me track my soil temperatures.

Cold frame growth in early spring.

Structures to Extend the Season

The most effective way to warm the soil is to cover it. Coverage on the surface will help a little but bringing that covering up off the ground so that the sun's rays get trapped inside helps much more. There are many ways to approach this, and each has its own pros and cons.

CLOCHES

Cloches are individual plant covers. Today, they tend to be more for ornamental or indoor plant terrarium use but having extra buckets or clear plastic totes available to add to individual or small areas of plants can be a lifesaver during cold spells. This is a great option if you only have a few plants that may need protection.

FLOATING ROW COVERS

Floating row covers can be used early in the season to add a small amount of frost protection to cold-hardy plants. Look for cloth called "reemay" or "agribon," lightweight non-woven materials that allow a high percentage of light and water through. They typically come in ten-foot-wide rolls in many different weights. The heavier the weight, the less light gets through. I tend to use these covers short-term, as long-term growing under these can invite pest infestations (unless you are using for overwintering when there are no insect pests). This cover does best when kept above the plants with sturdy wire hoops.

Checking on broccoli under floating row cover.

LOW TUNNELS

Quick, easy, and inexpensive to build, low tunnels are easy to pop up anywhere, so they work well with crop rotation. These temporary structures are miniature versions of greenhouses. The domed plastic is great at trapping and holding heat in the soil. These work both in the spring to warm soil for earlier planting and in the fall to keep cold-hardy crops in the garden longer.

DIY LOW TUNNEL

- 18"–24" sections of ¼" rebar (I use 6 total for my 4 × 8 beds)
- 8'–10' sticks of ½" PVC (I use 4 total for my 4 × 8 beds)
- 2–6 ml plastic sheeting (I use roughly 10' × 16' sheets for my 4 × 8 beds)
- Clips or blocks to secure plastic snug to ground

1. Start by finding the dimensions of what you want to cover, and pound in ¼" rebar every two to three feet along the perimeter, so it sticks out a few inches above the ground.
2. Then, slide ½" PVC over the rebar, arching from one side of the bed to the other.
3. Secure an extra piece of PVC along the length of the top to stabilize the low tunnel and help keep it from collapsing during snows.
4. Cover in plastic. Anything from two to six milliliters for the thickness will work. Rolls of plastic typically come in ten-foot-wide rolls, and I suggest planning for roughly double the width of your bed for

the width of the plastic. You can use clips to keep plastic in place, dig it into soil, or use anything handy like landscape bricks to hold it down. This does bring plastic into your garden but is reusable for many seasons to come. I've been using the same materials for many years.

COLD FRAME

Cold frames are permanent structures to create an insulated microclimate by capturing the sun's energy and extending the growing season. They can be constructed from wood, concrete blocks, and even hay bales, and they're covered with some sort of clear plastic or glass. They tend to heat up sooner and hold that heat a little better than low tunnels, depending on their construction. Pay close attention to the sunlight early in the spring, taking your cues on where to place your south-facing cold frame from the sunshine.

We built ours to fit some found windows, but if you are purchasing the "window" piece, I'd suggest no deeper than 3 feet as for at least part of the growing season there will be a window blocking access from the back. Our cold frame tends to increase the soil temperature by 10°F–20°F, giving us a great head start and extension to our growing season.

We also place succession sown seedlings there as a nursery, as it's an easy spot to drape a floating row cover. You can also insulate your cold frames with straw bales to keep them even warmer.

COLD FRAME TIPS

- You'll want at least two layers of lumber stacked upright, so you can angle the top layer to capture sunlight. The exact degree of the angle isn't critical but aim for between 25–55 degrees. Making the construction as airtight as possible will add to the effectiveness.
- Add hinges to your windows or plexiglass and you are set for easy access to early and late season planting and harvesting.
- Framing out the window pieces will allow you to prop them up at different heights to control the temperature throughout the season.

So satisfying to harvest late into the season!

DOUBLE COVERAGE

Eliot Coleman, a pioneer in organic and winter growing practices, coined the phrase "Persephone Days" for the winter days with less than ten hours of sunlight. Those darkest of days, dependent on your latitude, mean there's no growth, but a happy holding pattern under the protection of low tunnels. He also introduced the idea of double row covers. Coleman estimates that the double layers move your gardens one thousand miles south. I practice this when I place my winter sowing containers inside the cold frame (more on winter sowing on page 51).

Perennials for the Homestead

Perennials are plants that come back year after year. Many of our earliest and most anticipated harvests come from our gardens' perennial food plants.

Perennial foods take some time to establish and produce harvests, but that initial wait is repaid manyfold with less maintenance and increasing yearly harvests. Try to place them in the best spot for their long-term growth, anticipating other nearby plants and trees that will continue to grow as well.

Some of our favorite perennial foods are:

Asparagus: The first substantial food every spring. A single patch will last for a good twenty years.

Rhubarb: A farmstead favorite for its hardiness and reliability. It will grow for more than twenty years.

Horseradish: Known for avid spreading, it grows long, deep roots.

MICHELLE

PERENNIAL HERBS

Perennial herbs have a special place in my gardens and heart. They helped me fall in love with the power of plants back in my teens. They're also some of the toughest plants around. Herbs aren't too picky about where they grow. Many adapt to lower light conditions, don't require much space, and come with built-in pest protection. They're part of our daily lives from herbaceous salads all the way through the winter with sips of herbal tea.

Our must-grow perennial herbs include:

- Chives
- Garlic chives
- Lemon balm
- Mint
- Oregano
- Thyme

Jenny Saling
The Happy Herban
@the_happy_herban
Oakland, California

© Jenny Saling

Jenny is an urban gardener who works with private and corporate clients, helping them grow their own gardens. She grows food and flowers, but her special passion is growing her own herbal teas. She shares that every step of the growing process, from starting seeds or purchasing starts at your favorite nursery, to harvesting, drying, and sipping provides incredible benefits to body and mind. Think about flavors you like in a cup of tea, along with colors you like to see in the garden. Many herbs have beautiful flowers and crafting a tea that is pleasing to all your senses often provides the most benefit! Her biggest tip: Avoid drying herbs in the sun because they will burn and lose flavor.

JENNY'S FAVORITE BLENDS

- Lemon verbena as a perfect, single-herb cup (Jenny's favorite herb of all time)
- Chamomile, clover, and hibiscus
- Rosemary, cinnamon, and stevia

PERENNIAL HERB PROPAGATION METHODS

Rooting of stem cuttings: Take a non-woody stem, usually six to eight inches in length, and remove leaves from the bottom two inches. Place in water and change it regularly. Depending on the plant, you'll see roots in anywhere from one to six weeks. You can help the plants stay hydrated during this process by placing a clear plastic bag over the tops. Place in loose, well-draining soil once roots have formed. Water heavily and keep out of direct light for a day or two, as roots started under water can't absorb nutrients from soil right away.

Layering: Take a low-growing stem or branch and secure it gently to the ground. Cover the stem or branch with soil and wait for the plant to take root. You can "wound" or remove the underside of the stem to help rooting as well.

HARVESTING TIPS

When harvesting herbs, choose the healthiest leaves and stems, and herbs do best when harvested often—so don't hold back! Harvest in the morning, if possible, but not when leaves are wet. Many herbal guides tell you to pick before it flowers, and while there may be a difference in medicinal values, most people's palates can't tell the difference between herbs harvested before or after blooming. The pollinators sure appreciate the flowers, though!

VERY BERRY CROPS

So many fruits can be grown in your own yard. These perennials will give you years (and sometimes decades!) of sweet and juicy homegrown goodness. When choosing a berry variety, consider how you'll eat it: fresh or preserved. **Add some bird netting over the crops in summer to keep hungry birds from harvesting for you.**

Strawberries are an absolute family favorite. Keep them weeded and add a new layer of straw each year to keep the berries off the ground and you'll be enjoying these for years to come!

Blueberries like acidic soil around 4.5–5.5 pH to produce well. They are self-fruitful and have a gorgeous color.

Raspberries are a cane fruit that come in a wide variety of colors and seasonality. Pruning back old canes is part of the upkeep.

***Aronia* berry (a.k.a. chokecherry) + elderberries** are both sun-loving, tall shrubs that bear dark purple, astringent berries later in the season. We grow Aronia to use the berries in an immune-boosting syrup. **Please note that elderberries must be cooked before consuming.**

Currants + gooseberries are two low shrubs that grow well in partial shade and produce loads of small berries great for preserving.

Grapevines were a recent addition to our homestead, and they're so easy to grow and delicious! Seedless varieties are easier to enjoy fresh—unless you're ready to crunch those seeds.

FRUIT TREES

Nothing says "I'm a homesteader" like picking fruit from a tree in your yard! They're worth their weight in gold but take a few years to establish and start setting fruit. Many dwarf varieties exist, allowing for full-sized fruits from miniature-sized trees sooner. Dwarf trees generally grow from eight to ten feet high, semi-dwarfs grow to around fifteen feet high, and standard-sized trees are often well above twenty feet high when mature. Place in full sun and anticipate their mature sizing.

Pollination is another important factor when placing fruit trees. There are two ways fruit trees are pollinated, either by their own pollen, or by another genetically different variety, so trees are either self-pollinating (referred to as self-fruitful) or need cross-pollination (self-unfruitful). Since many fruit trees require another tree to cross-pollinate with, but often require very specific trees, it is best to start by finding the fruit tree you want to grow, and then matching the best pollinator tree. To have the best cross-pollination, resulting in the best fruit set, try to plant pollinator trees within fifty to one hundred feet of each other.

- Apple tree: Needs a pollinator
- Cherry tree: Self-fruitful
- Peach tree: Most are self-fruitful
- Pear tree: Does best with a pollinator
- Plum tree: Most need a pollinator

SEED STARTING

I'll never forget that aha moment I had after coming home from a vacation and finding that my pole beans had gone past prime picking. It dawned on me that these beans are still valuable because they'll grow more food for me next year . . . and so my seed saving journey began!

Starting (and saving) seeds tie us back to tending nature in ways both empowering and humbling. On a more practical level, growing your garden from seed provides a major cost savings. A packet of seeds is usually less than the cost of a single small potted vegetable or herb

Healthy tomato seedlings produce better crops!

start. Add perpetual savings if you can save the seeds that you grow. However, seed-starting equipment can add up fast. Like all things gardening, we recommend starting small!

GROW DIVERSITY

There are countless varieties of seeds to choose from compared to the limited variety of plants available to purchase in nurseries. You can select seed for differences like cold tolerance, days to maturity, and colors (to name a few).

TIMING

A common mistake new seed starters encounter is starting them too soon, myself included! Many companies suggest a number of days or weeks prior to your average last frost date for starting seeds. For my growing zone, 4b, the typical last frost date is generally mid-May, but this date is changing due to climate chaos. You can also start seeds a little earlier if you plan to transplant them out into the garden under cover. Learn more about growing under cover on pages 37–41.

A typical seed-starting schedule for different seed packets will have you starting seeds as early as ten to twelve weeks prior to the last spring frost, to just two to four weeks prior.

Seed Chart

Find seed information on how long a seed is viable, the best temperatures it will germinate at, the coldest temperatures the plant itself can tolerate, the average days to harvest, and whether it is best to start indoors or direct sow.

BEST SUCCESS FOR STARTING DIFFERENT SEEDS

- **Best to start indoors because they take a long time to get established:** celery, eggplant, leeks, onions, peppers, and tomatoes.

- **Best to start indoors if you want an early jump (especially northern gardeners):** broccoli, cabbages, cauliflower, chard, cucumbers, melons, kale, kohlrabi, lettuce, and squash.

- **Best to direct sow:** beans, corn, carrots, peas, potatoes, and radishes.

- **Best vegetables for winter sowing:** beets, broccoli, cabbage, cauliflower, chard, kale, kohlrabi, lettuce, and spinach.

Seed Starting Chart

	Years Seed is Viable	Germination Temps	Temp Threshold	Days to Harvest	Start Indoors	Direct Sow
Arugula	3	45°F–70°F	28°F	40–50		x
Beans, Dry	3	60°F–80°F	32°F	80–120		x
Beans, Snap	3	60°F–80°F	32°F	50–65		x
Beets	4	40°F–85°F	28°F	50–70	x	x
Broccoli	3	45°F–85°F	24°F–28°F	50–70 from transplant	x	
Cauliflower	4	45°F–75°F	26°F	50–70 from transplant	x	
Cabbage	4	55°F–85°F	24°F–28°F	60–95 from transplant	x	
Carrots	3	45°F–80°F	28°F	65–80		x
Corn	2	55°F–95°F	30°F	95–110		x
Cucumbers	5	65°F–95°F	32°F	55–65 from transplant	x	x
Kale	4	45°F–70°F	24°F	45–75	x	x
Lettuce	5	35°F–75°F	26°F	50–60	x	x
Melons	5	70°F–90°F	34°F	70–85		x
Onions	1	40°F–75°F	28°F	100 from transplant	x	
Peas	3	40°F–70°F	28°F	50–60		x
Peppers	2	65°F–85°F	32°F	70–80 from transplant	x	
Radish	5	45°F–80°F	30°F	30–40		x
Spinach	3	35°F–70°F	30°F	40–50		x
Tomatoes	4	55°F–85°F	34°F	70–90 from transplant	x	
Winter Squash	4	70°F–95°F	32°F	95–120	x	x
Zucchini	4	70°F–95°F	34°F	60–80	x	x

Seed-Starting Setup

A 1020 tray, heat mat, T5 LED grow light, and soil blocker are my seed-starting mainstays.

GROW LIGHTS

There are endless options out there for indoor grow lights and, like with most things, you get what you pay for. You can get regular fluorescent "shop lights" which are less expensive up-front, but there are specific benefits to different kinds of lights, including light quality (the wavelength or color) that mimics natural sunlight's full spectrum and intensity. For the general homesteader starting most plants, a full spectrum light of around 240W, or 5,000 Kelvin should do well. We use T5 LEDs and have been happy with the results. Keep in mind that a more efficient lightbulb will produce more light with less watts of energy.

A common complaint with seed starting is ending up with leggy plants. Placing the lights as close as possible to the seedlings helps keep them strong. Setting a timer so your lights can stay on between sixteen to eighteen hours per day is a good idea, too. Plan for enough space under your lights as your plants grow taller.

TRAYS + POTS

Before you get planting, sanitize the pots and trays you'll be using for seed starting by washing in hot soapy water and scrubbing off dirt, then soak in a bleach solution for a few hours (for an 8 percent bleach, use around one tablespoon per gallon of water). Rinse well and let air dry. This is an important step to fight the problem of seedlings damping off, which is when seedlings die back at the soil level due to fungus and bacteria in the soil.

The industry standard size for seed-starting trays is called a "1020" which is roughly 10" × 20". Please stay away from the super flimsy plastic trays. Think about how heavy pots will be with ready-to-transplant seedlings before your purchase. You can repurpose plastic containers or buy new pots.

SOIL BLOCKING

Soil blocking has been around for years but is gaining popularity because it grows great seedlings. Using a soil-blocking press, you pack soil into squares and press out a firm block of soil, removing the need for a pot. You then plant seeds directly into this block of soil. It holds itself together, creating the perfect environment for seedling roots to "air prune" and eliminating the problem of root-bound seedlings. This process reduces transplant shock and makes it nearly impossible to overwater.

I use a solid 1020 tray with a mesh 1020 tray nestled inside for my soil block seedlings. There is still plastic involved, but the process is more sustainable overall.

HEAT MATS

There is no single best temperature for seed germination, as it depends on the seed. There is a huge variation, with peas germinating in 45°F soil and beans preferring around 70°F, but in general you'll get a higher germination rate and quicker germination with the use of a heat mat, especially for many of the plants we typically start early: tomatoes, peppers, and eggplant. Heat mats are simple waterproof plug-in units that fit under a regular 1020 tray.

SEED-STARTING MIX

Always start seeds with a sterile seed-starting mix. Do not use regular garden soil or previously used potting mix, as these can harbor bacteria and fungus that can kill seedlings. There are many brands of seed-starting blends available, but I like to mix up my own blend. I get compressed bricks of coco coir which yield roughly 2.5–3 gallons from one compressed brick after soaking it in water and letting it expand for a few hours. Be aware that perlite dust isn't great to breathe in so mixing this outside or dampening the perlite before mixing is advised. This is my recipe for soil blocking and seed starting:

Planting Seeds

Seeds require air, water, and the right temperature to germinate. In general, seeds give you clues on how deep to plant them from their size. The bigger the seed, the deeper to plant. Tiny lettuce seeds get pressed into the top layer of soil, while bean seeds get pushed much further down into the soil. A general rule of thumb is to plant twice the depth or width of the seed size. Keep in mind some seeds need light to germinate, while others require darkness. Your seed packet should state any specific instructions. I like planting into already dampened soil and watering them in with a gentle sprinkle of water.

COVER

After sowing and watering seeds in, you'll want to keep them warm and damp to help germination. The simplest way to do this is to cover them. We've all seen the clear plastic domes to help keep in the humidity but reusing a piece of plastic wrap works just as well. Remember to remove any cover as soon as you see green popping up! Keeping the soil and emerging seedlings covered too long invites mold—a seedling's worst enemy.

WATERING

Just like watering plants in the garden, you're going to want to water the soil, not the leaves. And since we've got them in trays, we can even water from below. Watering from below helps water evenly and fully, so you'll also water less often which is better for root development. Watering from below also decreases "splash-up," the chance for fungal and mold (damping off) problems. There are systems you can set up for this, but I still prefer to hand water because it

Thinning seedlings to one plant per cell or soil block is a hard but important step in growing from seed. Only one of these tomatoes can stay.

gives me a chance to check on each tray. Let the top layer of soil dry out a bit, and keep in mind that more seedlings suffer from being overwatered than drying out!

The most important part of seed starting is simply paying attention to them daily. Luckily, this is also the part that brings gardeners the most joy: Tending to their babies, watching the daily growth, and responding quickly.

TIPS FOR KEEPING SEEDLINGS GROWING WELL

- Adding a fan will both help air flow, which will keep pests and diseases down, and strengthen plant stems. If you don't have a fan, gently run your hands over the plant tops to mimic the movement.
- When fertilizing seedlings, use a diluted (50 percent strength) form of organic

fertilizer once a few sets of true leaves are present, and only every four-plus weeks after that, if you haven't transplanted them out by then.
- Pinching off top growth and/or buds will help some seedlings (like flowers and peppers) grow stronger and produce more buds.

SEED-STARTING TROUBLESHOOTING

If your seedlings get pests (like aphids), try spraying them off with the stream setting on a spray bottle or take them outside and use a gentle hose setting. Make sure to set a fan in front of the seedlings to help them dry off as well. Air flow in general is helpful in seed starting.

Fungus gnats are becoming more and more prevalent in our seed-starting mixes. To combat, water with a diluted hydrogen peroxide mix (two to three tablespoons per gallon of water), top pots with vermiculite, use yellow sticky traps, and if they continue to get worse, consider watering or spraying the soil surface with a Bt (bacillus-thuringiensis) product. Bt is a naturally occurring bacteria that, once ingested, kills targeted insects.

You can also bake soil to kill any adults or immature fungus gnats. It's sort of stinky, baking soil, but it works. Set the oven temperature between 175°F and 200°F (no hotter than that), spread your soil in a thin layer on a cookie sheet, and bake for about an hour.

Moldy soil is another growing problem. I don't usually have this problem, maybe because I don't tend to overwater. I do know that mold likes warm, damp environments so removing heat mats and letting the soil dry out a bit will help. You can scrape off the soil with the mold on it, and then water with a diluted hydrogen peroxide mix.

HARDENING OFF

Hardening off is an essential part of growing healthy vegetable plants from seed. You'll need to slowly acclimate your seedlings to the full power of sunlight, wind, and changing temperatures. Find a partially shaded spot that's not too prone to wind gusts and start by bringing the plants out for fifteen to thirty minutes the first day, increasing from thirty to sixty minutes per day for at least a full week. Try to avoid the noon hour for the first few days as well. Not giving them enough time to acclimate can give them "sun scald" and set the plant's growth back by days or weeks.

TRANSPLANTING

Once fully acclimated to the outdoors, you can transplant when the soil is warm enough for the crop; as this varies depending on the crop, refer to the seed packet. Both soil and air temps need to be warm enough. **Now is the time to check out that garden plan you worked so hard on!**

I often transplant my tomatoes, peppers, and other heat-loving plants out under cover, giving them a little warmer soil and air and added protection against lower overnight temperatures. The best transplant day is a cloudy one but putting up a shade cloth helps lessen transplant shock. I fertilize at time of transplant with a slow-release fertilizer (see page 27 for my recipe), or a balanced mix containing N-P-K (nitrogen, phosphorus, and potassium/potash) ratios like 3-3-3 or 4-4-4.

GIVE IT TIME

When you transplant plants that looked so big in your seed-starting area into the garden, they tend to look tiny. They'll also take a day or two to bounce back from transplant shock. Try to give

them (and yourself) some grace and appreciation. Remember that this plant was a tiny seed not that long ago. And trust in nature, knowing that your tiny tomato plant will end up taking up all the square footage you let it.

Congratulations, you grew food from seed!

Winter Sowing

Winter sowing brings seed starting outside at the end of winter and is an eco-friendly option for those cold-hardy vegetables. This is when you plant seeds in an opaque or clear container such as a milk or water jug and set them outside. Seeds germinate in the containers when the temperature is right for them, and they are ready to plant out into your garden from there.

Trudi Greissle Davidoff is the pioneer of winter sowing. She introduced the idea as mimicking the natural cold stratification that many perennial seeds need to germinate. I start my winter sowing of vegetables toward the end of March here in zone 4. There are some obvious benefits to winter sowing: earlier seedlings, no hardening off, stronger plants, and no expensive equipment needed.

Drill holes in the bottom of your container.

DIY WINTER SOWING

- Screw gun with drill bit
- Box cutter
- Food-safe containers (think typical recycling items such as milk or water jugs, etc.)
- Damp potting soil
- Seeds of choice
- UV- and water-resistant garden marker
- Heavy-duty duct tape

1. Drill drainage holes in the bottom of each container.
2. Cut a hinge if needed (for access).
3. Fill each container with damp potting soil three to four inches deep.
4. Plant one or two types of seed in each container.
5. Label each container (inside and out) with a garden marker.
6. Tape the container closed with heavy-duty duct tape.
7. Place the planted containers outside (where they will get sun and rain). Watch for your seeds to germinate. Once seedlings emerge, watch their temperature and water needs closely. Open container after chance of frost is past. Transplant the seedlings into the garden once two sets of leaves have grown.

Make sure to label well. I add both inside and outside labels and dates.

Growing Microgreens

Microgreens are a fast, easy, and delicious way to keep growing your greens inside right through cold and dark winters. They pack ten to forty times as much nutrition as their full-grown counterparts. Microgreens include a wide variety of edible immature plants typically ready to harvest in two to three weeks. Certain varieties of greens, herbs, flowers, and vegetables lend themselves to this process. You do not eat the roots like with sprouts. You harvest by cutting above the soil level and eating the stem and leaves.

GETTING SET UP

Beginners often start by growing a single type of seed at time. Plants like broccoli, radish, or arugula tend to be the easiest-to-grow varieties. I also enjoy some premixed varieties for extra spice,

color, or flavor profile. Technically, you can grow any kind of seed as a micro, but buying the right seeds, sold for growing and being harvested as a microgreen, is much more rewarding. Grow lights will really help you grow great microgreens in the darkness of winter, which is when I crave them the most!

Keep in mind, a small amount of microgreens goes a long way.

PLANTING MICROS

- Place an inch or so of soil in the bottom of a tray and press it down so it isn't fluffy. Make it as smooth as possible. Keep in mind that soon you'll be harvesting, so deep soil isn't necessary.
- Dampen seed-starting mix. Scatter seeds on top of soil, so that they are almost touching

each other, making sure they have good contact with the soil but are not covered with soil. Some seeds also do better when soaked before planting. For example, pea shoots, which I soak for one day before planting.

- Spray seeds to moisten and adhere to soil, then cover with plastic wrap. Place a tray on top of wrap and place a weight on top, such as water bottles, books, or whatever fits.
- Remove cover and weight after two or three days once you see good growth. Water from below if needed. Place under a grow light.
- Keep watered until harvesting. I have found that mixing a small amount of hydrogen per-oxide into the water really helps keep mold down in my microgreen trays, too.
- Harvest by cutting (either with a sharp knife or scissors) above the soil level.
- Store them in the refrigerator in a sealed container with a damp paper towel without washing. Wash just before eating. Best if used within one week.

MICROGREEN FARMER
Amanda Yadav
Fiddlehead Farm
www.fiddleheadfarmmn.com
Andover, Minnesota

I first met farmer Amanda as a vendor at winter farmers' markets. She grows a diverse line of specialty produce which includes microgreens, edible flowers, and specialty leaves. She's active in her local community as a farm-to-table link and educates the community on health benefits of microgreens through hands-on classes.

© Amanda of Fiddlehead Farm

Amanda's #1 tip for new microgreen growers: If you see white fuzz in your microgreens, don't throw them away assuming it is mold! Microgreens can get white root hairs that look like mold. The best way to tell the difference is to spritz with water. Root hairs will fold down and disappear while mold will remain in place and look more like a spiderweb.

Biggest win: "I created a salad share with an option for 100 percent reusable packaging based off of increased customer requests for sustainability. While I expected it to be well received, I did not expect 97 percent of members to choose the reusable option! It is my hope that it encourages people to not only make changes toward sustainability, but to also not be afraid to let businesses know they want them!"

GROWING SPROUTS IN A JAR

STEPHANIE

Growing sprouts at home is incredibly simple and very inexpensive. They are tasty, nutritious, and add a delightful crunch to a sandwich, salad, taco, soup, or just eaten as-is. My mom has been sprouting seeds for decades and this is the no-fail method she taught me years ago.

Yield: 1 quart jar

- 1 tablespoon organic sprouting seeds (alfalfa, clover, mustard, radish, or a mixture of all)
- Cool water, as needed
- Cheesecloth, cut large enough to cover the top of the jar
- 1 rubber binder
- Patience (about 5–6 days' worth)

1. Add sprouting seeds to a clean quart jar and fill with cool water until the seeds are submerged. Add about 1 to 2 inches of water. Cover jar with cheesecloth and secure it with a rubber binder. Soak overnight.

2. After the seeds have soaked 12+ hours, pour out the water and rinse the seeds once more and drain. Cover the top of the jar with cheesecloth once again, and secure with the rubber binder. Turn the jar horizontally and slowly rotate the jar to spread the seeds out so that some stick to the sides of the jar. Store jar on its side in a dark place out of direct sunlight at room temperature, 60°F to 75°F (15°C to 23°C). You want to avoid the seeds clumping together, or they may mold. Repeat the steps of rinsing the seeds daily until the sprouts have grown 1 to 2 inches. It takes about 5 to 6 days until most sprouts are ready to eat, or 6 to 7 days for broccoli sprouts.

3. Once the sprouts have grown enough to eat, take the amount you want from the jar and continue to rinse daily for a couple of days and allow them to continue to grow on the counter as you use them. If longer-term storage is needed, give them a final rinse, and drain well. Place sprouts in a sunny window briefly, for 20 minutes or less, to allow them to turn a vibrant green. Wipe the rim of the jar with a clean, dampened, lint-free cloth or paper towel, add the canning lid, and tightly screw on the ring. Transfer to the refrigerator and eat within 2 weeks.

SEED SAVING

Just like growing your own food makes you appreciate your meals, growing from saved seeds will make you more deeply appreciate the entire plant world! Saving your own seeds can tune you into the reality that plant growth is a continual process. Knowing that you're planting a seed that you saved is a pretty great feeling, and it's even better when you taste the food that grew from that seed.

Until a few generations ago, most farmers and gardeners routinely saved nearly all the seeds they grew. Saving your own seed is empowering! You'll be continuing a seed-saving legacy that started with domesticated agriculture twelve thousand years ago. By saving the best of each crop, you'll create a better locally adapted plant each season. You'll save yourself money, plus have something of unique value to share with other homesteaders. I love a good seed swap!

Plus, there is no special equipment necessary, just something to hold the dry seeds. You can purchase seed-saving bags and sifters to save some time if you really get into it.

A WORD ON OPEN POLLINATED, HYBRID + GMO

Open pollinated plants are grown from seed that have been naturally pollinated, either through wind, insect, or self-pollination. Seeds saved from these plants will grow into the same plant again, known as "true to type." You can also think of this as meaning the seeds are "stable." If a seed has been grown for a few generations, it may also have the label of Heirloom. All Heirlooms are open pollinated; both are options for saving seeds.

Hybrid plants are bred from two (or more) different plants to create a new "hybrid" plant and flower/fruit/vegetable. Because the plant has multiple parents, planting saved seeds from hybrids will most often result in growing something that resembles one of the parents, or a mutant. Hybrid seed packets should be labeled with an "F1" which means it is a first-generation hybrid.

GMO (Genetically Modified Organism) seed is produced through a combination of traditional breeding techniques and genetic engineering to produce seed that has a specific "gene of known function." As far as I have seen, it is near impossible for the home gardener to purchase GMO seeds.

THE PROCESS

It can be simple and straightforward; save seeds from the best plants when those seeds are fully mature. Dry and store them until you plant.

Some seeds require cold stratification to germinate best. Cold stratification involves seeds spending an amount of time in cold temperatures, usually with freeze/thaw cycles to help break down the seed coat. This process aids in germination and is typically common only with perennials. You can check if seeds you are saving require this at your local nursery or online at seedsaversexchange.org or prairiemoon.com.

Did you know that saved seeds become acclimated to their growing conditions? This can give you better adapted plants in your garden in as little as seven years!

Basic rules of thumb are:

- Legumes (peas and beans) should dry on the vine.
- Solanaceae (tomatoes, peppers) can be harvested when fruits are ripe.
- Hold off saving seeds of anything from the cucurbit family like squash, cucumbers, and gourds unless well separated (like minimum half a mile!) because different varieties will likely cross-pollinate.

EASY SEEDS TO START SAVING

Beans + peas: Look for large, fully formed pods. Let pods dry on the vine, and it's okay to harvest after frost. Shell from the pod to help dry completely. Keep in airtight container once dry.

Lettuce: These seeds seem to take forever to fully develop and will look like hundreds of little dandelion flowers bursting into fluff when ready. I suggest using a seed collection bag (or tying netting) around the flowers to help contain the seeds as they develop. Once most of the seed heads have formed—you'll see some seed dropping off—you can then cut the stalk and place the entire head into a paper bag. Let it dry

This bolted lettuce plant has thousands of fully formed ready-to-drop seeds.

another week, then shake vigorously to remove fluff and seed heads. Then, pour into a bowl to start blowing and separating more fluff from seed. This process can take while, and since this is for your use and not "going to the fair," you can decide when it is clean enough.

Tomatoes: Choose large, healthy tomatoes. Harvest when fully ripe, then gently scoop out seeds and pulp. Tomato seeds are surrounded by a gel coating that stops them from sprouting inside the tomato and needs breaking down to germinate. We help that seed coat break down by fermenting the seeds. Submerge seeds in water, then cover the jar with a paper towel and let sit for two to four days. Seeds that float to the top are not viable and can be tossed. Once the seeds have sunk to the bottom and there's a stinky layer of mold on the top, the seeds are ready. I know, gross. I usually scoop off the top layer and discard, then rinse the remaining seeds, strain, and dry on paper towels. Store in an airtight container once dry.

Bell peppers: Harvest from large, healthy fruits that are fully mature. Pull off seeds from ribs, being careful not to damage the seed coating. Dry for a few days or until completely dry, then move to airtight storage.

Flowers for Seed Saving

I save so many flower seeds of both annual and perennial pollinator plants. This is where I see a *huge* cost savings. Those packets of filler seeds and four packs of annuals can really add up. Saving seeds of flowers is a great way to add loads of color and pollinator power to your gardens.

EASIEST ANNUAL FLOWERS TO SAVE

- Calendula
- Cornflowers
- Morning glories
- Marigolds
- Nasturtium
- Poppies
- Strawflower
- Mexican sunflowers (*Tithonia*)
- Zinnias

EASIEST PERENNIAL FLOWERS TO SAVE

- Aster
- Butterfly weed
- Gray goldenrod
- Meadow blazing star
- Milkweed
- Yarrow

Seed Libraries + Seed Swaps

Another way community and gardening go together! Seed libraries help locals "check out" free packets of seeds. A borrower checks out and plants a packet of seeds. They grow and enjoy the plants. The seeds ripen and gardeners harvest seeds from those plants and return a portion of them back to the seed library inventory. More seed libraries are opening every year. Search for these community driven gems online and you'll be surprised by what pops up!

No seed library near you? Seed swap!

SEED SWAP

Online gardening and homesteading communities are great for seed swapping opportunities, or maybe a local garden club holds a seed and/or plant swap. If not, you could organize a seed swap among a local group!

START YOUR OWN SEED SWAP

Start with deciding some basic parameters: types of seeds, how people will divide, label, and transport their seeds, where the swap will be held (a lot of table space is essential), what to do with unclaimed seed at the end, etc. Then, gather a list of names and send invites. You can make it as big or little as you like. Online seed swaps are here to stay, too. These open up a larger pool of people and seeds but require postage.

The best part of seed swapping or growing seed from a local seed library is the connections you'll make with the people and the plants. Seeds tell stories, and when we grow what we know, we become part of that story, too.

MN SEED
Courtney Tchida
MN SEED Project
northerngardener.org/mn-seed-project/
Roseville, Minnesota

The MN SEED Project started in response to seed companies running low on many native seeds during the pandemic. The MN SEED Project is a collaboration of the Minnesota State Horticultural Society, the Como Seed Library, and a local garden educator.

Together, they decided to focus efforts on teaching people how to save and share seeds from their garden. An invitation to a restored prairie in the fall of the first year has led them to two years of grant-funded work focused on creating an ongoing and interactive *Native Plant Community Science Project*.

Multiple seed collection events are held each year followed by community seed cleaning, processing, and swapping events. This has created a community of practice around seed saving and thousands of seeds now shared and grown across our region. Seed saving teaches the endless bounty of nature that we often overlook in our gardens.

Building community at a seed collection event. Left to Right, Amy Peterson of 21 Roots Farm, Michelle (one of the authors), Brittany Wiitala of 21 Roots Farm, Courtney Tchida of MN Horticultural Society, Stephanie Hankerson, a local garden educator, and Dawn Lamm of Como Community Seed Library.

Chapter Three
PRESERVING THE HARVEST

Some of the material in this chapter comes from the National Center for Home Food Preservation.

You'll thank yourself once you learn how to preserve food. There are many safe methods, which I will explain throughout this chapter. Personally, water-bath canning, dehydrating, and fermentation are my preferred methods for extending the harvest. Michelle utilizes her freezer and pressure canner more often than I. Which methods you choose to utilize are dependent upon what best fit your needs and interests.

You may think you need to put up cases of jars of food to make preserving worthwhile, but that's not true. Small batches here and there tend to add up. A spacious, sprawling kitchen is also not a requirement. I have been canning in my small galley kitchen for over fifteen years, and that says a lot considering I've written, developed, and tested recipes for all three of my cookbooks in this kitchen.

Preserving your own food gives you control of what you consume. Sure, you can easily go buy a jar of ready-made jam or pickles at the grocery store—but check out the ingredients on the label. A lot of already prepared foods are filled with food dyes, synthetic ingredients, and preservatives. Making and preserving food yourself allows you to control not only the flavor of the food, but also what additives are going into the food. Here are the ingredients on a jam label of a very popular jam maker that is found at most grocery stores nationwide: Strawberry Jam: strawberry juice, high fructose corn syrup, corn syrup, sugar, fruit pectin, citric acid. Would you prefer that over homemade strawberry jam that only requires organic strawberries and organic sugar?

For some, preserving food is more of a necessity than a choice. My husband, for example, cannot eat corn syrup because his body becomes inflamed from corn syrup, and with inflammation comes an increased risk for blood clots, and clots put him at risk of having another stroke. I have close friends that cannot feed their children food dyes because of the adverse reactions that the ingredients have on the neurobehavior of their children. So, for many, making it yourself makes the most sense.

One thing I learned while writing my first cookbook, *Can It & Ferment It*, that has stuck with me is freshly harvested produce water-bath canned within forty-eight hours of harvest actually has more nutritional value than raw produce found at the grocery store. What I'm saying is that after the freshly harvested food is canned and exposed to the high heat of the water bath, it still retains more nutritional value than a raw cucumber or other fresh produce found at the grocery store. This is because the produce at the grocery store could have been harvested weeks prior and it likely traveled across the country and could have been stored in a ripening room for weeks before ever hitting grocery store shelves.

Fruits and vegetables begin to lose vitamins as soon as they are harvested, so fresh is best whenever you have the choice. If you can't/don't garden but have farmers' markets or farmers available to you, that is your best option for the freshest foods since their produce has usually been harvested within twenty-four hours. When preserving, use organic produce whenever possible and always use produce that is not treated with food-grade wax sealant or harsh chemicals. **Wash all produce, supplies used, your preservation space, and your hands thoroughly before preserving, regardless of which method of preservation you're conducting.**

In addition to using freshly harvested foods, when selecting produce, be sure to pick fruits and vegetables that are not bruised or damaged. For some recipes it is beneficial to try and select produce that's uniform in size. An example would be when making pickles. Having uniformity allows the produce to pickle evenly, which will result in a consistent end product.

Farmers are happy to explain their farming practices and I have found that many fruits and veggies are indeed farmed organically, but the farmers have not gone through the process of making that official due to the cost incurred. Do not hesitate to ask farmers questions about their farming practices, because you might be pleasantly surprised by their answers. Remember to always ask when the produce was harvested to ensure freshness.

Throughout this chapter I'll summarize the methods used for preserving food and go a bit more in-depth about the methods I personally use throughout the year. To explain each method step-by-step would be an entire book itself. Read about the methods and what supplies are required and see which ones interest you most. Check Resources (page 131) to learn our recommendations for further education on these food preservation methods.

Food Preservation Methods + Explanations

There are several safe methods of preservation used to extend the harvest from the comfort of your own home, including the most popular methods: cold storage, freezing, dehydrating, water-bath canning, pressure canning, curing, smoking, and fermenting. My special interest lies in vegetable fermentation and water-bath canning, but I also do a lot of freezing and dehydrating and occasionally pressure canning, and I can't wait to get deeper into curing and smoking.

Water-Bath Canning

This is the method used for preserving pickles and fruit, and other acidic foods or foods that have been acidified with a pH of 4.6 or lower.

Once jars are filled with hot food, a warmed canning lid is applied, and the jar ring is twisted on. Then, the jars are submerged into the water-bath canner and the pot is covered with a lid. Once the water reaches a roiling-boil (to kill off any pathogens) a timer is set per the recipe. This method of preservation creates an airtight environment where the lid is vacuum sealed on the jar.

Water-bath canning is one of my most used methods for preserving food. I enjoy the process because it not only preserves food but retains the quality and great flavor of the food for years. Also, the canned food doesn't require any refrigeration until the seal is broken; it can be stored in a pantry, cupboard, or closet until it's opened. Plus, home canned goods make great from-the-heart gifts and are much less expensive than buying them from the store.

My students often tell me that they are afraid to begin water-bath canning because they don't want to harm themselves or others by poisoning of improperly canned foods. That's a very valid reason to be hesitant, but if the process is followed step by step and the recipes used are tested or developed by a trusted resource that followed the approved methods for home canning, then there is virtually no way to harm anyone.

Water-bath canning is used to process foods with a pH of 4.6 or lower. Acidic foods, such as fruit jams, pickles, and other preserves that have been acidified with vinegar, lemon juice, or citric acid will not be susceptible to botulism since botulism cannot survive in acidic conditions with a pH of 4.6 or lower.

Many years ago, I became a Cottage Food Producer in the state of Minnesota through the University of Minnesota Extension Food Safety Program. What this means is that I can make approved non-potentially hazardous foods and

Botulism is a life-threatening bacteria called *Clostridium botulinum* that is found in soil and on raw foods. The spores of botulism are not harmful until given the right conditions. The bacteria is found in low acid, anerobic, moist environments; however, it cannot grow below a pH of 4.6. Water-bath canning involves preserving acidic foods so, if preserved properly, there is no chance of botulism because of the foods' high acidity levels. Pressure canned foods are more at risk because they have lower acidity levels but the process of heating the food up to a minimum of 240°F, which can only be attained with a pressure canner, will destroy all the spores before they can become toxic. That is why it is extremely important to follow trusted recipes.

canned goods from home and sell them direct to consumer in the state of Minnesota. Since taking the class and obtaining my license, I have sold a variety of my canned goods each winter. Each fall I take a look at all of the preserves I have made throughout the season and select an assortment of jams, jellies, pickles, salsas and sauces to label and sell. It's a great way to earn some income while doing something I really enjoy from my homestead.

BASIC SUPPLIES FOR WATER-BATH CANNING

Many of these items you likely already have in your kitchen:

1. Large water-bath canning pot with lid and a rack, 21–33 quarts in size. These are typically sold in big box stores and online in a starter set. The rack is required to keep the jars off the bottom of the pot and allows water to flow around all sides of the jars. Canning

pots range from about \$20 to \$100. Read the range recommendations for each water-bath canner; some do not work with electric, glass-top ranges. If canning one single jar, a fourth burner pot comes in handy, as it comes with a rack to hold your jar off the bottom and heats quickly. Two small jars can be canned at the same time with a fourth burner pot, but there must be a barrier between the jars. These pots usually range between \$30 to \$50.

2. Wide-mouth/canning funnel.
3. Glass canning jars with new lids and rings (rings can be reused as long as they are not rusty or dented). To be safe, do not reuse jars from the grocery store that were commercially canned; that is a completely different process. Those jars can be used for other preservation methods such as fermentation, just not home canning.
4. Jar lifter. These are tongs made specifically for canning. They have a rubber or silicone coating over part to keep jars from slipping as you maneuver them. You will use them to clasp the jars when placing them into the hot canning pot and again when lifting them out after the boiling water-bath process.
5. Ladle. A ladle with a pour spout makes for even less mess when filling jars with sticky jam or pickling brine.
6. Measuring cups in a variety of sizes.
7. Measuring spoons in a variety of sizes.
8. Clean lint-free towels or paper towels to wipe the lips of the jars clean before adding the lid and ring.
9. Sharp paring knife.
10. Chopstick, butter knife, or canning tool to remove air pockets from hot- and cold-packed jars while filling them.
11. Large- and medium-sized thick-bottomed, nonreactive (stainless steel or enamel-lined) pots for making jams, sauces, and brines.
12. Candy thermometer, to measure the temperature of the water or jam/sauce. Not required but convenient.
13. Cutting board.
14. Salt. Canning salt, also known as pickling salt, is preferred; it is pure sodium chloride. Kosher salt is also acceptable, though the amounts may vary depending on the recipe. Be sure to consult a salt conversion chart when using a different salt than what a recipe calls for. Never use iodized salt.
15. Vinegar. Only use vinegars that indicate a 5–6 percent acidity level. Many bottles will note "pickling vinegar" on the packaging. I've personally only used store-bought vinegar because it offers reliable acidity results and I know it's safe.
16. Sugar. As you've probably noticed, canned jams, jellies, chutneys, and other sweet preserves generally include more granulated sugar than you'd expect. Sugar not only helps preserve the color of the food, but also helps the canned goods gel and become firm instead of syrup-like. The Ohio State University Extension Service states that sugar also acts as a preservative by inhibiting microbial activity; thus, recipes should not be modified or adapted. Brown sugar and honey can be substituted for granulated sugar in recipes, though it will not cut down the overall carbohydrate content. It is not promoted by the Extension Services to use artificial sweeteners when canning preserves. However, there are liquid and powder pectin options on the market that will help reduce sugar in recipes. If you purchase pectin to reduce sugar in recipes, please be sure to read the directions that come

with the pectin packaging to fully understand how to use it. Pectin can be found online or in the canning section of most supermarkets.

17. Water. The purest water you have available to you is the best option. I have a reverse osmosis system at home that I often use. Water with minerals such as iron could cause discoloration but is fine to use. I've canned with tap water from the city where I live for many years, and it's always provided great results. Some chemicals added to city water could possibly cause an adverse reaction to the end-product, but you may need to learn by trial and error to know if your tap water will work. If you are in a rural area and have well water as your main source, you can have the water tested to see if there has been any contamination. If you are unsure, store-bought water is an option.

If you live 1,000 feet or more above sea level, you'll need to increase the boiling time of the recipe you are following to ensure that is it safely preserved.

Sea Level	Processing Time
1,001–3,000 ft.	Add 5 minutes to the processing time
3,001–6,000 ft.	Add 10 minutes to the processing time
6,001+ ft.	Add 15 minutes to the processing time

© *Shutterstock*

Vegetable Fermentation

Fermentation for vegetables not only preserves food, but also makes it more nutritious in many ways because it offers the healthy-belly bacteria known as probiotics. Once fermented and stored in the fridge, fermented foods last nearly indefinitely. However, the tastes and textures continue to change even while refrigerated since the process of fermentation does not stop once cooled, it just slows way down. Ferments are generally best consumed within six months to one year, depending on which ingredients are used.

To ferment vegetables, all that is required is the produce you're fermenting and either salt (for dry salting) or salt and water (for brining vegetables). The fermentation process can take days, weeks, or even months, depending on the desired outcome and vegetables used. The process of lactic acid fermentation, also known as wild fermentation or lacto-fermentation, creates an acidic environment where bad/unsafe bacteria cannot survive and the good bacteria can thrive. The lactic acid preserves the texture, taste, and nutrients in fermented foods.

Fermented foods contain plentiful and varied probiotics which are beneficial to your digestive system. As fermented foods become more popular and more research is being done, scientists are finding that there is an important link between gut health and brain health.

BASIC SUPPLIES FOR VEGETABLE FERMENTATION

- Selection of 1-, 2-, 4-, and 8-cup measuring cups.
- Measuring spoons in a variety of sizes.
- Wide-mouth funnel for filling jars.
- Clean lint-free towels or paper towels.

- Sharp knife.
- Glass canning jars in quart and pint sizes, a fermentation crock, or other vessels made for safely fermenting.
- Jar weights for fermenting in jars (to keep the produce under the brine) or other larger weights if fermenting in crocks.
- Cutting board.
- Wooden kraut pounder/masher/damper (optional but helpful to pack your vessel with food).
- Salt. Coarse kosher salt is my favorite to ferment with because it offers great flavor and is inexpensive and easy to find. Sea salt is another great option for ferments, but the amounts vary due to the fine grain of sea salt. Refer to a salt conversion chart when using alternate salt options.
- Water. The purest water you have available to you is the best option.

FERMENTATION SUCCESS DEPENDS ON . . .

Brine is the liquid added to a ferment (salt dissolved in water) or the liquid that is naturally created by adding salt to a vegetable (dry salting) such as sauerkraut. Brine level plays a crucial role in the success of a ferment. The brine always needs to cover the fruit/vegetable that is fermenting by about ¼ to 1 inch of headspace. This keeps the ferment from being exposed to air and prevents mold from forming. Low brine level is the main reason ferments go bad, so be adamant about checking the brine level daily. If the produce in your ferment has floated above the brine, just push it back below with a clean finger or utensil.

Temperature plays a big role in fermentation. In my opinion, 60°F to 75°F (15°C to 23°C) is the ideal range for vegetable fermentation.

I like the flavors of my fermented food when fermented in that temperature range. Keep in mind that the warmer the room is, the quicker fermentation will happen; and adversely, the colder a room is, the slower the fruit or vegetable will ferment. I generally ferment most when my home is between 68°F to 72°F (20°C to 22°C), as this is the hot-spot range for ferments, in my experience. If you do not have air conditioning in the summer, consider leaving a covered ferment in the basement (if you have one) or a cool corner of your home. Otherwise, plan to do most of your fermenting during the cooler months of the year. You could even ask to keep your ferments at a friend's house; I've done it!

Freezing Your Harvest

Freezing is likely the most familiar modern-day method of food preservation to the masses. It's ideal for fresh vegetables, fruit, meat, and prepared meals. If packaged properly, freezing extends the life of the food for years. It is an excellent way to preserve the nutrition of the food and the process is very simple.

When I was in Hawaii for my Master Food Preserver Certification, we spent the majority of one of the days learning about freezing. I didn't think there was much to it other than putting items in containers, popping them in the freezer, and forgetting about them until I wanted to use them. But there is a lot more to consider if you want to extend the life of the food to its best ability.

It's important to have a reliable freezer that keeps food stored at 0°F or lower. Keep a thermometer in your freezer so that you can see if the temp rises for any reason. They even make freezer alarms that will sound if the power goes out or if the temperature spikes for any reason.

This is especially helpful to have if you have a stand-alone chest freezer.

Just like other methods of food preservation, you always want to use the freshest foods with the best quality available to you. Don't freeze any moldy or spoiled foods.

PACKAGING

Proper packaging makes all the difference in the world when it comes to properly freezing. If packaged properly, food can last many, many years in the freezer without getting freezer burn. Suggested packaging for freezing includes:

- Food-grade plastic containers with ridged sides.
- Butcher paper that is vapor-resistant.
- Freezer tape.
- Glass jars with wide mouths and straight sides. Keep in mind that jars with liquid require headspace. Pint-sized jars should have ½" headspace and quart-sized jars should have 1" headspace to give the contents room to expand when freezing. Loosely packed fruits or vegetables (such as beans or corn) without liquid don't require headspace.
- Plastic freezer bags which are specifically made for freezing.
- Vacuum sealing is an ideal packaging option for freezing since the process removes the air so well.

FREEZER BURN + THAWING FROZEN FOOD

Freezer burn happens when food isn't packaged properly and it loses moisture. The freezer burned portion often loses color and dries out. The freezer burned portion is still totally safe to eat, but oftentimes the freezer burn will cause an off taste, so it is recommended to cut away any freezer burned portions of the food before using.

Safe thawing practices include thawing in the refrigerator, in cold water, or in the microwave. The USDA Food and Safety Inspection Service recommends placing food in a leakproof plastic bag and immersing it in cold water for faster thawing. If the bag leaks, bacteria from the air or surrounding environment could be introduced to the food. Tissues can also absorb water like a sponge, resulting in a watery product. Change the water every thirty minutes or so to make sure it stays cold. Cook immediately after thawing.

It's also recommended that, if using the microwave to thaw, you should cook the produce immediately after since some portions of the food likely become warm or cooked during microwaving.

Please see the University of Georgia Cooperative Extension Service's recommendations for freezing vegetables at https://nchfp.uga.edu/publications/uga/ uga_freeze_veg.pdf (pages 3–6) and the FDA's recommendations for refrigeration and freezing at www.fda.gov/.

Cold Storage

Cold storage/root cellars are an effective way to store root crops, such as beets, turnips, carrots, and potatoes as well as many other fruits and vegetables. Cold storage keeps the temperature cool, generally between 32°F–60°F, and the environment humid (90–95 percent relative humidity). If you don't have a root cellar, the refrigerator is a great cold storage option, especially if you have a crisper drawer. Beets can be kept in the fridge for about six months and carrots for about four.

Drying/Dehydrating Food

Drying/dehydrating is a brilliant option for drying herbs, fruit, vegetables, edible flowers, and meat. Food is preserved by removing moisture so that it cannot spoil. Dehydrating can be done in a food dehydrator or an oven. Some food can even be dehydrated safely by hanging in a room or by drying in the sun, especially if you live in a desert climate.

Food dehydrators are our preference for dehydrating since they have reliable accuracy, built-in temperature settings, are low cost to run, and are easy to use.

Some dried foods can be eaten for up to one year if stored in an airtight container.

We tend to hang dry most herbs in small bundles, but if using a food dehydrator, it's

recommended that herbs are dried at 105°F and lower, or the flavor can be impaired.

Drying flowers is great for candle- and soap-making (see on page 115) but we also dry flowers to crumble into our chicken's nesting boxes, food, and treats (see on page 95). Flowers are recommended to dry at 110°F (43°C) if using a food dehydrator.

Pressure Canning

Pressure canning is used for preserving low acid food with a pH above 4.6 such as meat, beans, soups, broths, and vegetables. To safely pressure can low acid foods, the canner needs to reach a minimum temperature of 240°F. Botulism can successfully be killed at this high temperature.

When pressure canning, the filled jars are added to the pressure canner with a little water at the bottom. The pressure canning lid is locked on so that once heated, the pressure can build. The steam helps increase the temperature. The pressure canner must reach 10–15 PSIG (pounds per square inch of pressure measured by a gauge) and hold this temperature for a certain amount of time. Temperature, PSIG, and cook time will vary per recipe and are dependent on how you've packed the jar, the ingredients included, and the size of jars you are preserving with.

Once preserved, the jar of food is shelf stable for at least one year and up to two. However, just like with water-bath canned foods, the quality and texture of the canned food tend to degrade over time.

If you live 1,000 feet or more above sea level, you'll need to adjust the pressure in a recipe to ensure that your pressure canner is reaching the proper pressure to heat the canner enough to safely preserve.

Sea Level	Weighted-Gauge (Pounds of Pressure)	Dial-Gauge (Pounds of Pressure)
0–1,000	10	11
1,001–2,000	15	11
2,001–3,000	15	12
3,001–6,000	15	13
6,001–8,000	15	14
8,001–10,000	15	15

BASIC SUPPLIES FOR PRESSURE CANNING

- Dial gauge or weighted gauge pressure canner. Presto® and All-American® brands are trusted.
- Wide-mouth/canning funnel.
- Glass canning jars with new lids and rings (rings can be reused as long as they are not rusty or dented). To be safe, do not reuse jars from the grocery store that were commercially canned; that is a completely different process. Those jars can be used for other preservation methods such as fermentation, just not home canning.
- Jar lifter. These are tongs made specifically for canning. They have a rubber or silicone coating over part to keep jars from slipping as you maneuver them. You will use them to clasp the jars when placing them into the hot canning pot and again when lifting them out after the boiling water-bath process.
- Ladle. A ladle with a pour spout makes for even less mess when filling jars with sticky jam or pickling brine.
- Measuring cups in a variety of sizes.
- Measuring spoons in a variety of sizes.
- Clean lint-free towels or paper towels to wipe the rips of the jars clean before adding the lid and ring.
- Sharp paring knife.
- Chopstick, butter knife, or canning tool to remove air pockets from hot- and cold-packed jars while filling them.

Curing + Smoking Food

Curing and smoking are most commonly used for making cured meats such as ham, salami, and bacon. Bacon is also often smoked.

Curing primarily uses salt or sugar or both to draw moisture from the food. The salt inhibits most spoilage by reducing the water available for bacteria to grow. Once cured or brined, the food is often cold- or hot-smoked, which requires specific temperature control for extended periods of time. Cold smoking requires a temperature of 100°F or below and hot smoking controls the temperature between 150°F –200°F.

The smoking process not only gives the food a smoked flavor, but also kills off any bacteria. The smoke offers an antimicrobial effect on the food, so as the outside of the food dries, it reduces moisture, which limits the ability for bacteria to grow.

This USDA website is an excellent resource for up-to-date information on all approved methods of preserving food: nchfp.uga.edu/.

QUICK PICKLED ONIONS

Quick pickles, also known as refrigerator pickles, don't require any canning. Once put together, just store in the refrigerator. This method of pickling can be applied to pretty much any vegetable to make a pickle (though some will turn out better than others). Pickled onions are good on everything. Trust me and give them a try. You'll find endless ways to use up this flavor-packed condiment.

Yield: 1 quart

- 2 onions, red onions preferred (about 4 cups sliced)
- 10 black whole peppercorns
- 4 bay leaves
- 1 clove garlic (optional)

Brine

- 1 cup apple cider vinegar
- 1 cup water
- 1 tablespoon canning salt

1. Heat a small saucepan over medium-high heat with vinegar, water, and salt.

Simmer and stir occasionally until the salt has dissolved, then remove from heat.
2. Pack a clean quart jar with onion slices, peppercorns, bay leaves, and garlic, if using. Pour the warm brine over the onions and allow to cool for thirty minutes before refrigerating. Screw on the jar lid and tighten ring. Transfer to the refrigerator. Enjoy within 2 months for best taste and texture.

Other yummy quick pickle combos: radish slices with chive-infused vinegar, cucumbers, green beans, or even zucchini with garlic and fresh dill, beets with clove and a little sugar, hot pepper slices with garlic, and sliced carrots with rosemary.

© Shutterstock

INFUSED VINEGAR

Use infused vinegars to enhance the flavor of your meals! Infuse a vinegar with just one or several of the items listed below. Be sure all fresh fruit and herbs are thoroughly washed and trimmed of any bruised or flawed areas before using.

Yield: 1 pint

- Vinegar of choice (white wine vinegar and champagne vinegar are ideal for infusing as they have a gentle flavor compared to white distilled vinegar).
- 1 cup fresh fruit such as raspberries, strawberries, blackberries, cherries, blueberries, marionberry, huckleberries, skin of 1 orange, lemon, lime, or other citrus (no pith), pomegranate, peach, plum, red/black currant, fig. Gently bruise fruit before adding to jar.
- 3 tablespoons dried herbs such as oregano, tarragon, rosemary, basil, dill, sage, spicy peppers (crushed), cinnamon, or lavender
- 3 sprigs fresh herbs such as oregano, tarragon, garlic clove, rosemary, mint, chives, chive blossoms, basil, dill, sage, fennel, spicy peppers (halved), or ginger.

1. Cleanliness is imperative to a successful vinegar infusion. It is required that jars are sterilized before use. To sterilize jars, first wash all parts of the jar (lid and ring as well) with warm soapy water, then boil the jar(s) in a hot pot of water for ten minutes. Keep the jar(s) warm until ready to fill with vinegar. Place the jar lid(s) in a small saucepan and heat gently until use.
2. In a small nonreactive saucepan, heat vinegar of choice from 190°F to 195°F, just before boiling point. Place fruit or herbs in a warm, prepared jar. Using a funnel, carefully ladle or pour the warm vinegar into the prepared jar, leaving ¼ inch of headspace. Wipe the rim of the jar with a dampened, clean, lint-free cloth or paper towel and again with a dry towel. Place the jar lid over the rim of the jar and tightly screw on the ring. Once cooled completely, store in a dark cool place for 4 weeks as the flavors infuse.
3. Once the flavors have infused to your liking, transfer to the refrigerator for storage. If you want to remove the solids, use a fine mesh strainer to strain out the solids and rebottle them in a new, freshly sterilized jar. Label and date. Store in the refrigerator for best freshness and flavor. Use within 6 months.

This method of infusing vinegar follows the rules and methods of the University of Georgia Cooperative Extension Service. If any mold or yeast occurs, throw out the vinegar. If any signs of fermentation occur (cloudiness or sliminess), discard vinegar. Your hands, prep area, and supplies must be clean, as harmful bacteria can survive in some vinegars.

Chapter Four

BACKYARD CHICKEN KEEPING

Our Chicken-Keeping Stories

First off, we're so excited that you've decided to join the ranks of crazy chicken people raising hens in their backyards! Just like gardening, there are as many ways to raise hens as there are backyards, so think about how this information can be applied to your own homesteading situation and use it as you will. As you'll see, the two of us do things differently, and while our differences come down to preferences, the foundations stay the same.

STEPHANIE

We thought about raising chickens for a decade before we made the leap. It felt like a massive undertaking because there was so much unknown. Setup is definitely the most laborious and costly part of chicken keeping, but once you've done that, it's very simple to raise chickens.

I had no idea that chickens ate mice until Smarty Pants, our Gold Star hen, popped out of the lilac bush with a mouse dangling out of her mouth. In shock, I picked her up and snapped a couple pics to show the fam what a good huntress she was but once I set her down she ran off, shaking the mouse like a ferocious dog, and down the hatch it went. My jaw dropped. Smarty Pants remains our mouser. In general, chickens are fantastic at pest control. They eat beetles, grubs, scorpions, ticks, and all sorts of pesky buggers. I find great pleasure in picking cabbage moth caterpillars off my broccoli and feeding them to my ladies. When they hear me holler "chicken treats!" they come running.

Truths abouts raising backyard chickens: They poop a lot, and it stinks, their poop attracts flies, they are loud—especially after laying an egg—and they will destroy your landscaping and gardens if given the chance. On the flipside, chickens can bring a lot of joy to your homestead with their silly antics, sweet cuddles, stellar pest control, and, of course, their (almost) daily gift of delicious fresh eggs.

It's our recommendation that you speak to your neighbors before you set out on a chicken-keeping journey. Make sure that they understand what's in store and that they are on board. I've found that neighbors enjoy the gifts of eggs and take pleasure in watching the chickens scratch around the backyard. We even sometimes move them up to pens in the front yard, where passersby like to stop and watch them, ask questions, and even bring their children back by to see. But we do keep them contained within fencing in the back and front because most neighbors would not find joy in their gardens being demolished in the blink of an eye by these little monsters.

Chickens tend to not have any boundaries whatsoever. They love to scratch up mulched garden areas if I'm not looking (hey, I can't blame them, there are a lot of bugs within the mulch) and they are very sneaky and go for what they want as soon as they have the opportunity. That's why it's important to have fenced off areas for them to safely roam in. I use cheapo fencing to keep them out of my garden beds and only plant chicken-friendly plants on the perimeters of the gardens so that if they do get in the back garden space, they can help themselves to the kale, lettuce, broccoli leaves, and chard. One thing to keep in mind about gardening with chickens is that a lot of flowers are poisonous to chickens, as well as dogs and cats. Before we got chickens, I researched all the plants in my yard and either removed or fenced off all the unsafe ones, which included ferns, rhubarb, lilies, irises,

tail

comb

ear lobe

wattle

crop

vent/cloaca

and milkweed. Make sure what you're growing is edible and safe for your pets!

MICHELLE

We really can't imagine our yard or our homestead without our hens. Throughout my twenty years of raising chickens, I've experienced so many situations, yet I'm still learning about them (and from them) today!

We've had lots of mixed breed flocks over the years and enjoy having a variety of hens. For us, raising calm and curious chickens is more important than the amount or color of eggs. But the variety of egg colors is definitely a fun bonus!

We've enjoyed many kinds of Orpingtons, along with Speckled Sussex, Easter Eggers, and Barred Rocks. We haven't had good luck with the Gold/Red Star breeds, which are all "sex-linked"

varieties. These are bred for egg laying and tend to get sick more often and die younger.

Our flocks help us reduce our food waste and close the loop by eating extras from the garden and kitchen, adding nutrition back into our vegetable gardens while providing delicious, highly nutritious eggs, not to mention all the chicken entertainment and soft feathery snuggles.

We are lucky to have a few hundred square feet for them to roam free under trees and shrubs with a fully fenced-in backyard for lots of safe scratching. Plus, lots of maple leaves get dumped in their area, which creates a layer of mulch and help keep them busy searching for new sources of bugs and worms. They have access to the compost piles as well, so we have to cover those piles if want to keep them from digging through those. It is an evolving adventure right in our backyard.

Chicken Breeds for Backyard Homesteaders

First off, we have to say that we've never met a chicken we didn't like. The best backyard birds tend to be more docile, cold- and heat-tolerant, have good egg-laying production, and don't have extreme needs for free-ranging space.

Some hens mature faster, meaning you'll start getting eggs sooner. Many of those breeds also lay more eggs per year, which means they'll stop laying sooner as well.

Some hens are twice the size of others. If you want smaller birds, look for Bantam varieties, although the Bantams are in general a little feistier and a little slower to start egg laying. Some breeds are known to get broody and just want to hatch those eggs (I'm looking at you, Brahmas and Cochins).

STEPHANIE

Be sure to investigate what your city codes are regarding roosters where you live. Technically, we can have roosters in our city, but if the neighbors complain, we must rehome them. We accidentally got a male chick, whom we deeply adored, but when he started crowing (which could be heard from blocks away), he was forced off the island.

Chicken Codes + Changing Them

Before you jump into chicken keeping, be sure to look up your local city ordinances. Each city has varying rules regarding the location of coops, the number of fowl you're allowed to keep, the type of fowl you're allowed to keep, and butchering laws. Some cities even require inspections to be conducted before providing permits to allow keeping chickens.

HOW I CHANGED MY CITY'S CHICKEN ORDINANCE

MICHELLE

If your city doesn't currently allow the raising of backyard chickens, don't worry. My city never used to either, but I got to help change the city ordinances, and I'd love to help you try, too! It was one of the most rewarding experiences I've ever been through and am still known as the "chicken lady" in my town because of this.

Start off by doing your research and find out if there's been a vote on this issue before, and if so, how recently. Call around to other nearby cities and find out their current ordinances, along with when and how those changes happened.

The keeping of chickens is governed by municipal ordinances (as far as I've encountered) and can be changed through a city council vote. So, you'll need to figure out who your city council person is and contact them. They're typically good at listening to their constituents.

Example of vetrap on splay/spraddle leg. © Lisa Steele

Remember, they work for you! They'll also give you a good idea of how the current council members feel about chickens.

Then, your council person adds the item to the meeting agenda. This is where it can get nerve-wracking for those of us not used to speaking in public, especially if there's opposition (which there was at my council meeting). Have a list of benefits and examples of others keeping chickens to strengthen your cause. Invite local experts and others interested in chicken keeping to attend and speak at that council meeting.

The council members will listen to all speakers, then discuss among themselves, and vote on the issue. Our council decided to license the chicken coop instead of the birds. This addressed some concerns about the structures and setbacks, along with ensuring a one-time involvement from the city, as opposed to annual licensing with paperwork to be filed and kept track of by city employees.

The civic experience was a wonderful way to get involved in my local food movement, and best of all, we've had hens and their eggs ever since!

Raising Chicks

MICHELLE

Raising your own chicks gives you the chance to have them really bond with you. You'll get to watch your chicks' personalities grow in the first few weeks, and it is such a unique experience. Take time to hold them and play with them when they're young and they'll be lap chickens forever. **Always wash your hands after handling chickens since chicken poop is a source of salmonella.**

CHICK HEALTH ISSUES TO WATCH FOR

There are a wide array of health issues that can arise with chicks, but here are some of the most common to watch for:

Pasty bum/pasty butt/chick pasting is when droppings stick to the chick's vent and the tail flap covers the vent (chicken butt) so that it cannot excrete waste. This can be caused by illness, stress, or even something the chick ate. To remedy, wash the vent area with warm water or use a warm cloth to hold on the bottom of the chick. Gently wipe away the poop. Repeat as needed until the chick resumes normal-looking droppings.

Respiratory issues such as trouble breathing, coughing, or wheezing. This could be caused by an unclean brooder. To remedy, clean the brooder thoroughly, wiping it down with a damp towel or diluted white vinegar, and replace with clean bedding and a clean waterer/feeder. Make sure the temperature is warm enough for the chicks.

Splay/spraddle leg is when the chick has trouble standing and its legs go off to the sides. There are many causes for this and it's a tough one to remedy. First, make sure the bottom of the brooder isn't slippery by layering the bottom with paper towels under the pine shavings. Causes for splayed legs include lack of nutrients, improper temperatures in the brooder or during incubation, or just born that way. Lisa Steele of FreshEggsDaily.blog recommends using a ¼"-wide, 5"-long piece of vetrap bandaging to hobble the chick's legs.

If the condition is detected while the leg and foot muscles are still growing and strengthening, it has the best chance for correction. Otherwise, the chick will not be able to get food and water and will inevitably pass away. Lisa says to loosely wrap the bandaging around each leg, connecting the ends in the middle about one inch apart (normal width apart) in sort of a figure eight. The chick should also be kept in a separate enclosure until it learns to stand. If the correction works, it will happen pretty quickly. Check the chick's progress twice daily and discontinue wrapping once the chick can stand and walk on its own.

BRINGING CHICKS HOME

You can order chicks direct from hatcheries and receive day-old chicks in the mail. This seems hard to believe but it works because chicks hatch with built-in energy stores. You can also pick up chicks from a local farm supply store if you want the opportunity to pick and choose exact birds. You can even go for the full experience of hatching your own chicks at home with an incubator! Regardless of which route you take, you'll need a brooder (a safe place to raise your chicks). Simply set up any tall-sided box/bin in a warm, draft-free area, with a waterer, feeder, and heat source.

Layer the bottom of the brooder with a nonstick surface. We prefer newspaper under paper towels for the first week or two. Avoid using just newspaper as the main layer, as this is *really* slippery for the chicks' itty bitty chicky feet and can cause leg issues down the road. Switch to newspaper with pine shavings on top once they know the difference between food and bedding, usually around two to three weeks old. Get the larger size pine shavings, not the small size, or else they will certainly eat them!

Supplies for Raising Chicks Inside the First Six Weeks

PROVIDE HEAT FOR CHICKS

Use a heat lamp/chick-safe heater or light bulb to keep the chicks at 90°F for the first week. A thermometer can be added to track the temperature. If the chicks are huddled under the lamp, they likely want it warmer. If they're hanging out away from the heater, it may be too warm. Each week you can reduce the temperature by 5°F until the temperature inside the brooder is the same as your room temp (about 70°F).

The chicks can be brought outside on nice days for a short "recess" when temperatures are similar to their indoor environment but be sure to keep them contained within fencing or a run. Avoid windy and rainy days during the first six weeks.

Consider fire risk when choosing which heating option is best for you.

FOOD + WATER FOR CHICKS

Feed new chicks a high-protein chick starter feed for the first six to eight weeks. They'll benefit from a chick grit as well, to help them digest food. Keeping poop and pine shavings out of their chick-sized feeder and waterer is the hardest part in the beginning.

Treats can be introduced after the first few weeks. Start with some chopped salad greens. There's nothing cuter than watching them zoom around after a little piece of lettuce. Dried

meal worms or soldier fly larvae are a great high-protein treat option too, but keep treats in moderation; never feed them above ten percent of their daily food intake.

TRANSITIONING TO THE COOP

After four to six weeks (as temperatures cooperate) you'll be ready for chicks to move out of your house; they grow quickly. Chicks, even at a couple months old, are still quite small and determined to explore their surroundings so check for possible escape routes. Make sure you've got a solid source of food and water; they'll eventually need a larger sized waterer and feeder once they're in the coop. At this point, the chicks will begin to eat grower feed until around eighteen weeks. Then, you'll switch to layer feed.

Tip: If you want to skip the chick phase altogether, there are places such as www. heritagepullets.com that sell pullets at about fifteen weeks old. Chickens start laying at different times depending on the breed, but generally around twenty weeks.

Coop + Run Setup

COOP PLACEMENT + STYLE

Preferred placement for the coop and run would be a space in your yard that has at least one side that is blocked from wind, a location that's partly shady, and a space that does not pool with water when the snow melts in the spring or during heavy rainfall.

Whether you build your own coop or buy a premade one, predator protection and protection from the elements is of the utmost importance. When selecting your coop, be sure to consider the weather conditions in your climate, the space you have for the hens to roam, and the durability of the structure.

If you live in the northern climate like us, it is common for temps to drop to negative 30°F or 40°F. Therefore, we need to make sure we either have an insulated coop and/or some sort of heater to help keep the hens safe from frostbite during the extreme cold spells. Good ventilation is also very important for the chickens in both the summer and the winter.

There are many coop plans available online if you want to build your own coop and run. The size of the coop you need will depend on how many chickens you intend to have. Buying a used coop is another great option for saving a few bucks. People get very creative with their coops. My friend's partner converted an old shed into their coop. One of our Instagram friends crafted hers from an old wooden swing set. Another friend turned their old gazebo into a coop.

Regardless of which route you take, make sure to give the chickens plenty of space because overcrowding can lead to fighting between the flock. Generally, you'll want at least a couple square feet of room per chicken.

Consider the types of predators where you live. Here in Minnesota, even in the first ring suburb that we live in, we must watch out for opossums, raccoons, cayotes, birds of prey, neighborhood cats and dogs, foxes, and rodents. There are even more predators as we get out of the city such as bobcats, weasels, bears, and snakes. You will need to create a coop and run that protect your flock from whatever predators are in your area.

Michelle's chicken tractor.

When we started raising chickens at our current homestead, my husband built this chicken tractor. A chicken tractor is a moveable chicken run that can be rolled from one location to another in the yard. It takes the power of chicken poop and literally spreads it around. If managed properly this can revive a lawn or prepare a space for planting. The trick is timing; don't let hens graze so long that they wipe out the vegetation (unless that's what you're going for). Also, if planting food crops into the area, give the chicken poop a good four to six months to decompose before planting. This design is a smart combination of a compact use of space; a pull-out floor for easy cleaning, and easy-to-access nesting boxes.

Suggestions for Chicken Coop + Run

- **Nesting box(es).** It is standard that there is at least one 12" × 12" nesting box per four hens.

- **A roost inside the coop for chickens to roost at night.** They'll appreciate other roosts around the setup as well (if possible).

We have two additional roosts that are made from sturdy branches that fell from trees on our property.

- **Bedding**: Options include pine shavings, straw, or other nontoxic chicken-safe bedding.

- **Enclosed chicken run** (if free ranging isn't possible or allowed) with enough space for at least ten square feet per chicken.

- **½-inch hardware cloth** to line the perimeter of the coop/run and dig twelve inches into the ground around the coop/run to keep predators from digging underneath. You can also bury hardware cloth under the coop/run instead.

- **Sand for dust baths** or sandy soil that the chickens can scratch and sprawl in. Dust baths are pest protection for the chickens (from parasites such as mites and lice). They also absorb excess oil from chicken feathers.

- **Container to store chicken feed** in and keep predators out of. We use a metal garbage can with a lid.

- **Age-appropriate feed.** Starter feed for the first eight weeks, grower feed for chicks up to eighteen weeks or so, and layer feed for hens eighteen weeks and older.

- **Chicken waterer and feeder**. There are many options to choose from, preferably up off the ground. Supply fresh water daily.

- **Oyster shells** or ground eggshells for hens of laying age since they benefit from the extra calcium.

- **Grit** or access to sand/dirt, depending on how often your chickens free range or if they have access to the ground. Since chickens don't have teeth, they store grit in their gizzard, and it helps them process the food.

- **Fly traps.** Flies are attracted to the coop, so we place fly bags outside of the run (not inside of the coop or pen).
- **Mouse/rat traps.** Chicken feed lures in a lot of rodents. We use traps that will not hurt our chickens or other animals if stepped on. They simply close when a mouse is trapped, not harming it. We normally only put them out in the winter since this is when mice are more likely to try and find a warm home with the hens.
- **Bushes or tree cover for added safety** when free ranging or somewhere to hide from predators if they fear an attack from hawks, owls, or eagles.
- **Motion sensor lights** (optional). Solar lights are a great option.
- **Coop odor-eater granules** (optional) to neutralize the ammonia and other smells from your flock.

General Flock Care

STEPHANIE'S BACKYARD COOP SETUP

When we were trying to figure out which setup to go with, we knew that our city only allowed three hens and they also required that we be outside with them whenever they free range. We also have dogs and a lot of predators in the area, so we wanted the hens safe and enclosed in a strong run whenever we weren't out with them.

After researching whether to build our own coop or buy a premade one, we found a brand called Formex that makes snap lock chicken coops. What drew me to this type of coop was that it doesn't require tools to put it together, making setup easy and quick. The coops are made from heavy-duty double-walled polyethylene plastic, which is considered to be one of the safest plastics and is highly durable.

The coops are maintenance free, have good adjustable ventilation, and offer easy access to collecting eggs. The plastic it's made from is waterproof and UV-resistant and even claims to be bear-proof! We don't have bears where we live, but I figured that if this coop was safe from bears that it would be safe enough to stand up against any of the predators we do have here.

We placed our setup in the northwest corner of our yard, which is partially under our silver maple and cedar trees. The trees offer shade and protection. The north side of the coop is protected by my neighbor's garage. Instead of adding a run to this coop, we put it inside of an 8 × 8 rust-resistant steel poultry pen.

We added ½-inch hardware cloth up the sides of the perimeter of the poultry pen and dug it into the ground. We also lined bricks and large logs around the perimeter of the pen for an additional layer of protection and bought a cover for the roof to keep the rain and snow out. The total we spent on the coop and poultry pen was $1,200. Our setup is long-lasting and strong against the extreme elements we have in Minnesota and safe for our little flock.

This setup allows us to leave the coop door open overnight during the spring, summer, and fall. We do close it if severe weather is predicted. Otherwise, the hens can freely wake up and go to bed on their own accord. In the winter, however, due to the temps and risk of mice looking for a warm spot, we do manually open and close the inner coop door at sunrise and sunset. There are

Stephanie's backyard coop setup.

auto-doors that can be installed to open and close coops if you are unable to do this yourself.

We decided on the breeds of our hens by the weight they'd be as adults and their tolerance of cold temperatures. Since our coop was only made to fit four hens, we decided to go with smaller breeds that would grow up to be around five pounds, and that would do well in our climate. We ended up with a Gold Star, a California White, and an Ameraucana Easter Egger. From these three hens, we get nearly eight-hundred eggs per year which are colored blue-green, white, and brown.

MICHELLE'S BACKYARD COOP SETUP

We had raised hens before in a few different situations, so being able to start from scratch was really fun!

Our city licenses the coop instead of the hens, so we had a few requirements to meet in the structure, including an overall size ensuring a minimum of four square feet per hen. My husband is a carpenter-turned-supervisor, so he's enjoyed building a few different coops over the years. Because construction prices fluctuate, we aren't able to pin down a cost, but suffice it to say, these are not cheap to build.

Michelle's backyard coop setup.

Our first smaller chicken tractor was great for our first four hens, but we eventually reverted to a coop we built for a different property for more hens because we liked having more space for them on those cold winter days when they are literally cooped up inside all day.

We like the metal roofing and sturdy lumber construction. It holds just enough heat and keeps out drafts without being insulated in our winters, while bringing through enough air flow in the heat of summer. We placed it under a plum tree for added shade protection against the summer heat waves.

Adding a fully enclosed run area made of hardware cloth on the bottom two feet allows us to leave the coop door that leads to the run open during nice weather. That said, making sure all the fencing and door latches are critter-proof is important. We like the latch style that slides and drops into place—not even racoon hands can manage those!

Keep It Clean

STEPHANIE

Keeping chicken coops clean is fairly low maintenance when you have a smaller flock. I only have three hens and besides keeping their food and water fresh, we only need to clean out the coop once a week to keep the odor under control.

To clean, we remove the soiled bedding and add new bedding in the coop weekly. The soiled bedding goes into our compost bin to be turned into nutrient-rich material that we'll later use in the gardens. Once a month during the warmer months, since our coop is made of hard plastic, I take it out of the poultry pen and give it a good scrubbing, rinse it down with the hose, and let it dry in the sun.

MICHELLE

We love keeping lots of fresh straw in the coop year-round. It makes for happy hens and easy cleaning. It also makes for great compost piles! We love our "coop poop plate" for helping to contain chicken droppings and easier clean up. A poop plate is simply a board or metal plate placed a few inches underneath the main roosting area for your hens. Since hens hang out on their roosts a lot, and poop while sleeping, the poop plate catches most of the poop inside our coop, which we scrape clean every few days.

We do a deep clean in early spring and again in late fall where we sweep and wipe everything down with a vinegar solution. We make sure to do the deep cleanings on warm, dry days to make sure the coop is ready for the girls again in the evening.

When we had poultry lice, I also dusted my hens and specific coop areas with a permethrin poultry dust. While this is a part of a synthetic pesticide and not organic, I felt it was needed. I use it very sparingly, and always with a mask. It is highly toxic to cats and honeybees, so be aware of those risks as well.

Tending to Sick Chickens

BACKYARD EMERGENCY KIT TO KEEP ON HAND

If you decide to get your own backyard chickens, you will at some point face a sick or injured one, so it is helpful to know which signs to watch for and to have a first aid kit on hand for such emergencies. Being prepared for the less-fun parts of chicken-keeping will help with the anxiety of nursing your little friend back to health.

SIGNS THAT YOUR FLOCK MAY BE SICK OR INJURED

- Pale combs or wattles, though this is normal in winter months when they are molting (the annual process when chickens lose their feathers and grow new ones).
- Unusual poop, such as diarrhea or mucous in droppings.
- Feather loss, not including when they are not experiencing their annual molt, which usually occurs in the fall.
- Lethargy.
- Discharge in nostrils.
- Hard or distended crop.
- Trouble walking, standing, or balancing.
- No appetite.
- Sneezing, coughing, or wheezing.
- Eyes looking sunken in, closed, cloudy, inflamed, or otherwise different than usual.
- Feces on feathers near vent area.
- Black spots or bugs on vent area.

EMERGENCY ITEMS

Here is a list of what we find helpful to have on hand when emergencies arise:

- Disposable gloves.
- Epsom salt for soaking injuries like when a chicken is egg-bound or dealing with vent gleet.
- Dog nail clippers for trimming nails that get too long, or beaks if need be.
- Styptic powder for applying to minor cuts or broken nails to help stop bleeding.
- Vetericyn Plus Antimicrobial Poultry Care to spray on cuts and wounds.
- Garden and poultry dust to use against mites, lice, or a maggot infestation. It is a permethrin dust, so wear a mask when applying and use caution.
- VetRx for respiratory problems.

- Sav-A-Chick Electrolyte and Vitamin Supplement for Poultry aids in hydration when the chicken is ill or during events of extreme heat or other stress.
- Organic apple cider vinegar to add to water when there is a sign of illness. This adds healthy probiotics with just 1 tablespoon per gallon of water.
- Poultry wound spray made with tea tree oil.
- Yeast infection cream for treating vent gleet on adult hens.
- Petroleum jelly or coconut oil. Apply to combs and wattles to help avoid frostbite when the temperatures reach -1°F or below.
- Syringe for hand feeding medications or water if need be.
- Vetrap bandaging.
- A dog kennel or other private and safe space with spare feeding/drinking supplies to isolate your chicken during recovery if need be.

Our friend and chicken expert Anne Kuo, author of *The Beginner's Guide to Raising Chickens*, offers one-on-one consulting services to help you troubleshoot any problems that may arise with your backyard flock. More info can be found at her website: www.realhensofoc.com/book-online.

Winter Care + Extreme Heat Care

Chickens are really good at keeping themselves warm. They are covered in feathers, after all! They are incredibly adaptable creatures, but if you live in the north like we do, temperatures can dip far into the negative degrees which is why we need to take some extra steps to keep them happy and healthy all winter long.

Keeping chickens over the winter really comes down to keeping them dry and out of the wind, along with offering them plenty of food and water. Like at any other time of year, being with your hens and knowing their routines are the best lines of defense.

HOW TO KEEP YOUR FLOCK WARM + SAFE

Use **heaters** when needed. Heating the coops is a point of contention for some chicken owners because doing so can hinder your flock from getting acclimated to the winter temperatures. Heaters also pose a fire hazard with a cord near or on the ground. You may think you've got the cord tucked away, but chickens are curious and have lots of time on their wings to investigate the addition to the coop, so please be watchful if you add one.

We both use flat panel radiant heaters to keep our coops about 10°F warmer than the temperature outside when the coop is closed overnight. We use only during the extreme cold of Minnesota winters and 10°F is not a large enough temperature difference to interfere with the chickens' temperature acclimation.

Good ventilation and a dry coop are important because you do not want moisture to build up; this would aid in frostbite and other health issues. As air gets colder it loses its ability to hold moisture. Add in the fact that chicken poop also contains urate (what mammals pee separately) and you've got a high percentage of moisture to deal with.

Most people keep three to six hens in a relatively small space in urban/suburban settings. So, let's imagine it's winter and your hens have been cooped up all night. They go outside to one of those 0°F mornings. When you add in a little windchill, the dampness surrounding their combs quickly becomes frozen, and you've got a hen with frostbite within minutes. A dry coop becomes obviously important.

Protect coop and/or run. Stack up straw bales on the sides of the coop or the run, hang plywood or hard plastic to the run's walls, or add tarps. Using an old shower curtain or leftover garden poly as an extra layer of protection from wind and snow lets light in while keeping wind and snow out.

Additional bedding. We both use a thick layer of straw in the coop and run over the winter and pine shavings in the cooler months. Whichever bedding you choose, use more than you would in the warmer months. You'll also want to make sure that all the chickens can comfortably fit on a roost up off the ground, as sleeping on the floor is colder and invites disease.

Heated waterer (optional). The heated waterer is an additional expense that you may not want to pay for, but it sure makes life easier. A two-gallon, plug-in, nipple-style drinking system keeps water from freezing, even on the coldest "Arctic Blast" Minnesota winter days. It can be hung from the top of your poultry pen and can easily be removed to refill. Check that the water is flowing daily once you open the hens in the morning, just in case a fuse blew, or it quit working for any reason.

MICHELLE

We use a simple waterproof heating pad under our regular waterer once the temperatures hover around freezing so that the hens don't have to peck through ice to drink because, well, they won't! Please do not put an open topped heated waterer inside your coop. This is a disaster waiting to happen. Chickens will get wet, and wet equals cold.

Adding a tablespoon or two of apple cider vinegar to their water a few times a week is another way I keep my flock healthy all winter long.

I also keep greens growing in my garden as late as possible for them as a great source of extra calcium. Ripping at big leafy brassica greens also gives them something to do when most of their foraging spaces are dead and brown. Once the fresh greens are gone, I dip into my frozen stash for treats.

LIGHT SOURCES

Adding a light source for dark winter days is up to you; there are pros and cons to both decisions. Stephanie doesn't supplement light

at her homestead, but we tend to use a regular light bulb (in a cage) to add both a little heat and light hours to their days. Chickens naturally slow down and speed up their laying with the sun's cycle. Adding light keeps chickens laying eggs more consistently during darker times of the year. We usually set an automatic timer to go on an hour or two before normal sunrise during the darkest months.

I recommend adding light in the morning rather than at night because a light that suddenly goes off might catch a hen off guard. This means a hen could spend the night on the ground (they may not jump to a roost in the dark) and will end up more stressed as a result.

FROSTBITE + COMB CARE

MICHELLE

The bigger, thinner, and more ridged the comb, the easier it is to get frostbite. The tiny, barely-there pea combs hardly ever get frostbite because they have good blood supply and are close to the head. Big floppy combs may need some extra care in a typical Minnesota winter.

When the temperatures plummet, I bring out a small jar of coconut oil (petroleum jelly works, too) to have ready for my morning visits to the coop. Coating the chicken's combs and wattles creates a waterproof barrier between the skin and the cold. Not very insulating, but it keeps the moisture and frostbite away.

Treating frostbite centers around managing the pain and possible infection. If a chicken does get frostbite they will recover, but it is painful for them. First, let the chicken warm up slowly, and don't apply direct heat to the area with frostbite. Monitor for infection daily. This is when being able to handle your hens to easily check on their combs, wattles, and feet becomes important. Look for swelling and heat but know that if a piece of comb does fall off a scab will form over it.

HOT WEATHER CARE

Sav-A-Chick Electrolyte and Vitamin Supplement for Poultry aids in hydration when the chicken is ill or during events of extreme heat or experiencing other stress.

Add a water mister if possible or spray water into the run and on the perimeter of the run/coop for the hens to step through to cool down.

Install a box fan for airflow.

Add additional shade if possible. Stephanie grows cucumbers and other chicken-safe vining plants on a trellis on the south side of the poultry pen during the summer months. This offers shade during the peak sun time of day and even an occasional snack if any of the fruit grows into the poultry pen. She also has a clothesline post near the coop, so she ties an old sheet from the poultry pen to that post to create shade.

Anne Kuo, author of *The Beginner's Guide to Raising Chickens,* is located in Orange County, California, and shares these additional tips:

- A large, shallow wading pool set in the shade is quite helpful because the hens not only drink from it for extra hydration, but also wade in it to keep cool.
- In a baking dish or other freezer-safe container, chop fruit and vegetables, fill with water, and freeze to create ice blocks. This will not only keep the chickens cool while they eat the treats, but it will also keep them busy.
- Make sure the chickens have plenty of ventilation in their coop and run. Open coop

door and nest boxes allow for cross ventilation during the day so that the air is not so stifling warm in the night.

- For climates with extreme heat, you may want to install a special swamp cooler fan (evaporator coolers) or simply hang a damp towel in front of a fan.

Homemade Treats for Your Flock

We like to jazz things up with different snacks and treats for the hens. We especially like to incorporate treats in the winter, when our ground is covered in snow and frozen solid. Here are a few of our favorite treats that we occasionally make for our adult laying hens. Please note that treats should be given in moderation.

FRUIT + VEGGIE GARLAND

STEPHANIE

Celebrate the holidays with your hens or celebrate "just because." Start with good strong string or wire, then find a tool to push the string or wire through your garland ingredients. My hens love brussels sprouts, brassica leaves, grapes, apples, zucchini, cucumber, lettuce, squash, strawberries, and watermelon. I make a large needle out of wire, but a screwdriver or large sewing needle would work as well. Michelle uses a fishing stringer because it comes with a built-in needle and she ties it on the outside of the pen so that the needle end is outside of the cage, away from the hens.

Tie a knot in the string with at least a 6" tail and begin threading a variety of garland ingredients. Cut larger produce into 2" to 3" chunks. Keep the garland 18" or shorter so that it doesn't get too heavy, then tie another knot,

SUET TREATS

This is a great high-protein, high-fat treat that will keep your hens busy.

- ½ cup unsalted nuts, chopped (pine, pecan, pistachio, or peanut)
- ½ cup unsalted seeds (sunflower, pumpkin, chia, or sesame)
- ½ cup dried unsweetened fruit (cranberry, apple, blueberry, apricot, raisin, or banana)
- ½ cup dehydrated vegetables + herbs (carrot, zucchini, oregano, basil, or dried non-toxic flowers such as marigold or calendula)
- 1 cup scratch mix
- 1 cup coconut oil

1. Mix dry ingredients together in a bowl.
2. Melt coconut oil in a small saucepan on low until liquified. Use a heat-safe glass or metal baking pan as the suet block mold (large enough to fit 3 cups of mix), and line with parchment paper. I personally prefer to use silicone soap molds for my suet blocks (ones only reserved for suet and other food), since the set suet bricks easily pop out without the trouble of lining them with parchment paper.
3. Fill the prepared mold(s) with the dry ingredients and slowly pour the liquid coconut oil over the mixture. Allow this to cool and set for many hours or move to the refrigerator to speed up the process. The coconut oil will harden and turn white once completely cooled.
4. To serve, simply give the suet block to the hens or hang it in a suet feeder. It's best to avoid serving on very warm days, as the coconut oil will soften and melt.

leaving at least a 6" tail. Attach the garland to the chicken wire/fencing and watch the hens enjoy their special treat.

Be sure to keep an eye on the hens while they eat and remove the string/wire once they are finished snacking. String is unsafe for chickens to consume.

PURINA® FLOCK BLOCK® COPYCAT RECIPE

This is a great way to boost their protein and keep hens busy during the months when their foraging areas are covered in snow. A busy hen is a happy hen! The specific ingredients aren't as important as a general ratio of wet to dry. You can add in leftover quinoa or stale whole grain breadcrumbs. Chickens aren't picky.

- 2 eggs
- ¾ cup molasses
- ½ cup coconut oil or other oil that is solid at room temp, melted
- 1 cup crushed peanuts or peanut butter
- ½ cup dried fruit (raisins or other chicken-safe dried fruit), chopped
- 2 cups regular feed
- 2 cups cracked corn and/or whole oats
- 1 cup rolled oats
- 1 cup corn meal
- ½ cup ground clean eggshells

1. Preheat your oven to 350°F and grease or line your pans with parchment paper using whatever shape/size you want.
2. Mix wet and dry ingredients separately first, then together. The consistency should be thicker than a brownie batter. Push it down into the corners of your pans and flatten it out. Firmly pressing helps it hold its shape and keeps the hens pecking longer as well.
3. Bake for 45 minutes until it is dark and comes out solid.
4. Make this recipe into two blocks and freeze one for later.

FERMENTED FOOD

The first time I made fermented chicken food was when our hen Phyllis cracked her beak. She couldn't peck the way she normally did because it would induce bleeding. I decided to add water to her food and let it soak up overnight. I quickly noticed that the hens were extremely enjoying this softened food. Little did I know that I was not only making the food easier for my hens to eat, but also making it more beneficial for them. I learned in Anne Kuo's book, *The Beginner's Guide to Raising Chickens*, that by fermenting chicken feed, it allows the naturally occurring bacteria to unlock the grain's nutrition—making their enzymes, proteins, and nutrients more readily available for the body to absorb—just like in fermented foods that humans eat. She goes on to say that studies show that fermented chicken feed has many benefits, including better intestinal health, stronger immune systems, shinier feathers, increased egg size, less smelly droppings, and stronger disease resistance, including resistance to salmonella and E. coli. I don't solely feed fermented feed to my hens; however, I ferment one quart on a weekly basis, and they very much appreciate it.

little bubbles or even foam-like bubbling occur at the top of the ferment. Use a clean spoon to stir down the feed, as it will push up toward the mouth of the jar during the fermentation process.

The fermented feed may have a sour smell, which is another normal sign of fermentation. To serve, pour the fermented feed into a clean dish for your flock as-is or stir in any chopped fruit, veggies, leafy greens, oyster shells, or treats as you see fit. Discard if mold is present.

HIGH-PROTEIN MOLTING TREAT

It's obvious when my flock is approaching molting season because they begin instinctively trying to boost their protein intake. They search through my landscaped gardens and spaces where they normally learn to stay out of during the summer because they know many bugs hide within the mulch. At this point, I help them by lifting pots and stones around the yard so that they can peck and scratch the soft soil full of insects hiding below. I also help them by making high-protein snacks such as this recipe.

This is another recipe that I generally don't measure; I just add a little of this and a little of that. But here is the general outline that I follow: Cook one egg per 2 hens and scramble with coconut oil and one chopped garlic clove. Stir eggs into ¼ cup cooked oatmeal. Mix in ¼ cup high-protein wheat (hard red winter wheat berries, or other mixture of wheat) and seeds (black oil sunflower seeds or sesame seeds). Top with brewer's yeast and dried grub worms or black soldier fly larvae.

BENEFICIAL HERBS + FLOWERS TO GROW FOR CHICKENS

All herbs and flowers mentioned are beneficial dried, crumbled up, and sprinkled into their coop, food, and/or nesting boxes.

HOW TO FERMENT CHICKEN FEED FOR A SMALL FLOCK

Measure 2 cups chicken feed into a clean quart-sized glass canning jar. Add water until the feed is covered with at least 2 inches water and stir well, adding more water as needed throughout day 1 so that the feed stays submerged.

Cover with canning jar lid and ring and tighten. Ferment at room temperature, ideally between 60°F–75°F (15°C–23°C) and keep out of direct sunlight. Ferment between 1 to 5 days.

Burp the jar daily by unscrewing the lid briefly to allow built-up gas to release (and avoid possible jar breakage) and screwing it back on tightly. It is completely normal to see

after all so it's best that you know what is safe and what isn't.

Here is a short list of common items for your flock to avoid: mushrooms from the yard, potato leaves and green potatoes, tomato leaves/plants, onions, rhubarb leaves/rhubarb, fatty foods, high-sugar foods, salty and greasy foods, caffeine and alcohol, moldy and spoiled foods, raw beans and runner beans, and uncooked pasta or rice. The list could go on and on, so if you are unsure if what you are feeding your chickens is safe, do a little research on your specific plant in question.

- **Mint** helps repel rodents and insects, is safe for chickens to eat, and said to be calming for chickens.
- **Oregano** is a natural antibiotic and immune booster and is a guard against a whole host of common chicken illnesses.
- **Basil** promotes a healthy respiratory system and a healthy immune system overall.
- **Lavender** is a natural stress reliever and also an insect repellent. It can be chopped into food fresh or used dried.
- **Calendula and marigolds** both support healthy digestion. If eaten, they enhance the chicken's egg yolk, beak, and feet colors.

FOODS TO AVOID

Chickens can eat a surprisingly large range of food. However, as mentioned earlier, there are many things that will make them sick, including ferns, rhubarb, lilies, irises, and milkweed. In general, chickens are pretty good at avoiding what can harm them, but they have bird brains

All about Eggs

The breed of the hen will determine the number of eggs it lays annually. I get around eight-hundred eggs a year with just my three hens. Contrary to popular belief, you do not need a

Molting might look horrible but is perfectly normal for chickens.

rooster to get eggs. You need a rooster to have chicks; a rooster fertilizes the eggs.

Chickens also do not lay eggs year-round, unless they are supplemented with light during the winter months (hens need at least fourteen hours of light per day to keep laying), in which they will lay except when they are molting. A molt is when the feathers fall off and are replaced by new ones. Since feathers are made mostly of protein, the hens will not lay during this time. Molts usually begin in the fall and can last months.

The color of the egg depends on the breed. Chicken eggs come in gorgeous shades of white,

blue, green, pink, cream, brown, and even black. Young hens, called pullets, start laying between eighteen to twenty-four weeks, depending on the breed.

HOW TO STORE EGGS

Eggs that have natural bloom on them (ones that have not yet been washed) can be safely kept at room temperature for up to three weeks. Once they are washed, they need to be stored in the refrigerator. Per the USDA, eggs can be refrigerated for three to five weeks. That being said, I still keep my eggs in the fridge because the quality of the egg does begin to diminish each day that it is not cooled. If my fridge space is full already, I tend to leave unwashed eggs on the counter as needed until I have space. Date egg containers to keep an idea of age.

HOW TO WASH EGGS

Per the USDA[1], to destroy bacteria that may be present on the surface of the egg, wash the eggs in hot water, then rinse in a solution of 1 teaspoon liquid chlorine bleach per ½ cup water.

HOW TO FREEZE EGGS

Freezing eggs is a great long-term storage option. They will keep fresh for up to one year once frozen.

Wash the eggs and crack eggs individually into a dish. Stir each egg with a fork and pour into a plastic freezer bag. Be sure to date the bags and note how many eggs you have added to each bag.

Instead of using freezer bags, you can pour the mixed eggs into a silicone muffin tray and freeze the tray. Once frozen, the egg "pucks" can

1. www.fsis.usda.gov/food-safety/safe-food-handling-and-preparation/eggs/shell-eggs-farm-table#:~:text=Use%20only%20eggs%20that%20have,per%20half%20cup%20of%20water

be removed from the silicone molds and added to one large freezer bag and stored.

Frozen eggs are great for baking with but not so much for scrambling or enjoying as you would a fresh egg. Eat frozen eggs within one year for best quality.

HOW DO YOU KNOW IF AN EGG HAS SPOILED?

If I'm not sure about the quality or age of an egg, I do an old egg test that my mom taught me when I was a kid. I submerge the egg in a dish of water and if the egg floats off the bottom, it is an indication that the egg is old. Air pockets within the egg increase as time passes, so the larger the pocket is, the older the egg is. If the egg does not float off the bottom, it is perfectly safe to eat. The egg could still be safe if it floats but you'll have to crack it open to find out. Smell it. If it has an off smell, it has spoiled. An off odor and unusual appearance are your indicators.

EGG APPEARANCE

The following information has been taken from the USDA website.[1]

- **Blood spots** are caused by a rupture of one or more small blood vessels in the yolk at the time of ovulation. It is totally normal and completely safe.
- **A cloudy white** (albumen) is a sign that the egg is very fresh. A clear egg white is an indication that the egg is aging.
- **Pink or iridescent egg white** (albumen) indicates spoilage due to *Pseudomonas* bacteria. Some of these microorganisms, which produce a greenish, fluorescent, water-soluble pigment, are harmful to humans.

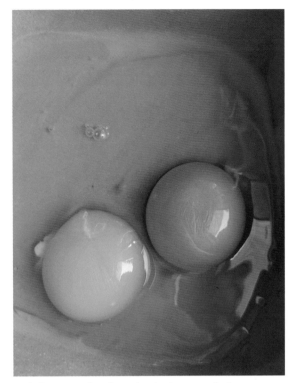

Left shows store-bought and right shows our fresh egg.

- **The color of yolk varies in shades of yellow** depending upon the diet of the hen. If she eats plenty of yellow-orange plant pigments, such as marigold petals and yellow corn, the yolk will be darker yellow than if she eats a colorless diet such as white cornmeal.
- **A green ring on a hard-cooked yolk** can be a result of overcooking. It is caused by sulfur and iron compounds in the egg reacting on the yolk's surface. The green color can also be caused by a high amount of iron in the cooking water. Scrambled eggs cooked at too high of a temperature can also develop a greenish cast. The green color is completely safe to consume.

WHAT HAPPENS WHEN YOUR HENS ARE PAST EGG-LAYING YEARS?

Chickens only lay at their full capacity the first couple of years; their production dwindles as the years pass. Once your hens stop laying, it is time to decide whether to keep your backyard hens as pets, rehome them, or *otherwise*. There are plenty of people that are willing to take older chickens off your hands. They are still great at pest management, after all, and there are also rescues that are happy to take older hens that have quit laying.

The option of eating them is pretty much off the table because older hens have tough meat, unless you slow cook the meat to tenderize it. Plus, the flavor of older laying hens is commonly off-putting for most people. Though, it's your decision if you decide to use them for meat. If you specifically want to raise chickens for meat, there are meat hens that grow quickly and are ready to harvest within a couple of months or less. However, some cities restrict butchering, so if you do decide to go this route, be sure to check your city ordinances first.

Regardless, a chicken's life will inevitably come to an end whether we want to think about it or not. It's good to have an end-of-life plan even before you begin your chicken-keeping journey. There are humane ways to euthanize a sick or suffering chicken and many veterinarians will also help the process along if it's something you aren't able to do yourself.

A Few Favorite Egg Recipes

BETTER-THAN-BOILED STEAMED EGGS

Fresh eggs are incredibly difficult to peel smoothly. The egg membrane sticks to the shell more when it's fresh so, when peeled, the cooked egg white often peels away as well. I tend to save my older eggs for hard boiling, since the air pocket in them has increased over time and they are easier to peel cleanly. However, there is a trick to cooking easy-to-peel fresh eggs and we can't wait to share it with you!

Get a pot with steamer basket set, add a few inches of water, and bring to a boil. Add fresh eggs at room temperature, cover, and steam for 8 to10 minutes for soft-boiled, 12+ minutes for hard-boiled yolks.

Prepare a bowl of ice water and transfer the steamed eggs (tongs recommended) from steamer to ice water bath to cool quickly. Wait until cooled and crack shell gently but try to break the membrane right away. Enjoy within one week. The leftover peeled eggshells can be crushed up and fed back to your hens for a healthy calcium-dense treat!

ONE MINUTE MAYONNAISE

This is such a liberating staple to make with all real ingredients. Most other homemade mayo recipes call for a food processor and yield much larger quantities. The trick to making this recipe work is using a wide-mouth mason jar that is just bigger than a stick blender. You can substitute many different oils. I have had good luck with avocado oil but you can use a blend of avocado, olive, untoasted sesame, and coconut oils. Use what you've got!

Yield: 1 cup finished mayo

- 1 large (or 2 small) raw egg(s) at room temperature
- 1 tablespoon lemon juice, lime juice, or raw apple cider vinegar
- 1 tablespoon Dijon mustard
- 1 pinch salt
- ¾–1 cup oil

1. Place room temperature egg(s), citrus or vinegar, mustard, and salt in your jar and add oil(s) to the top.
2. With the stick blender blades over the yolk, keep the blender firmly on the bottom of the jar and start blending. You'll see the oil and egg emulsify before your eyes. Keep blending for around one minute and once most of the ingredients are blended, you can raise the stick blender up a little to incorporate any oils.
3. This will not feel quite as thick as store-bought mayonnaise until after you refrigerate it. You can add more vinegar, mustard, or salt to suit your tastes with each new batch. Best if eaten within three weeks.

Step 2 of making mayonnaise.

LEMON CURD BY LISA STEELE

Lisa Steele of Dixmont, Maine, is a fifth-generation chicken keeper and creator of the popular website Fresh Eggs Daily. *She's the host of CreateTV's* Welcome to My Farm *and author of six previous books on raising backyard flocks. Lisa's latest work is an egg cookbook titled* The Fresh Eggs Daily Cookbook. *Here is Lisa's personal recipe for lemon curd, one of the most delicious and creamy treats. This recipe can be made with lemons, limes, grapefruit, or oranges in place of lemons.*

Yield: About 3 cups

- 6 eggs
- 1½ cups granulated white sugar
- ½ cup fresh squeezed lemon juice
- 1 stick unsalted butter at room temperature, cut into ½" cubes

1. Set a medium heat-proof bowl over a saucepan of simmering water. Whisk the eggs and sugar in the bowl until smooth, then add the citrus juice and whisk to combine. Continue to cook, whisking constantly for several minutes, until the mixture is warmed through.
2. Then, begin to whisk in the butter, a few cubes at a time, whisking in between each addition until the butter melts completely.
3. Once all the butter has been incorporated, continue to whisk, cooking until the curd thickens (about 15 to 20 minutes) and coats the back of a spoon. If you have a candy thermometer, this should happen right around 180°F–190°F.
4. Once the curd has thickened to a nice consistency, remove from the heat and spoon the curd into clean canning jars.
5. Let cool, then screw on the lids and refrigerate.

Sweet and tart lemon curd is a true treat!
© Lisa Steele

Lemon curd is wonderful on toast or an English muffin. It can also be used to fill cupcakes or tarts, cream puffs or donuts. Or you can eat it right off a spoon from the jar.

SPICY PICKLED EGGS

Yield: 1 quart-sized jar

Spicy Pickled Eggs

- 1–2 jalapeños, sliced
- 10–12 hard-boiled eggs, peeled
- 2 cloves garlic, chopped
- 2 teaspoons red pepper flakes
- 4 sprigs fresh dill

Brine

- 1 cup water
- 1 cup white distilled vinegar (5 percent acidity)
- 1 tablespoon canning salt

1. Add all spicy pickled egg ingredients to a clean quart jar, wedging the jalapeño slices between the eggs. In a small nonreactive saucepan, prepare the brine. Bring all brine ingredients to a simmer and stir until the salt has dissolved. Remove from heat and cool slightly.
2. Using a funnel, carefully ladle or pour the brine over the eggs until they are completely submerged. Wipe the rim of the jar with a clean, dampened, lint-free cloth or paper towel to remove any spillage. Place the canning lid on the jar and tightly screw on the ring.
3. Once the jar is no longer hot to the touch, transfer it to the refrigerator. Allow the eggs to pickle at least 1 week (if you can help yourself), but ideally 2 weeks before eating. The longer they pickle, the more flavor they will have. Eat eggs within 4 months for best flavor and texture.

For a less spicy version of this recipe, use the same brine ingredients and method but season with 1 tablespoon pickling spices and 1 tablespoon thinly sliced yellow onion instead.

Typical maple tapping setup with spile, hook, and collection bucket.

Chapter Five

SMALL-SCALE MAPLE SUGARING

We lived in our home for about seven years before we realized we could tap our maples. I always assumed that I'd need a forest to produce enough maple syrup to make it worth my time, but boy was I wrong. We have one small sugar maple in our backyard and one very large silver maple. Though sugar maples are ideal for tapping since they have the highest sugar content, there are many other types of trees you can tap such as birch, black maple, red maple, black walnut, sycamore, and box elder. Different types of trees offer different sugar content and can vary in sweetness and flavor. The best trees to tap based on sugar content are sugar maple, black maple, red maple, and silver maple. The lower the sugar content, the longer the boiling process will take.

Our silver maple is large enough to tap three spiles into. Our one large tree will produce enough sap to boil down into enough maple syrup to stock us up for the entire year, plus have enough to share with family and friends. Granted, we don't use a large amount of syrup annually, so we don't need to produce more than a few quarts or a couple gallons to make it stretch the year.

MICHELLE

Transforming sap into syrup is one of our family's favorite spring traditions. There is something invigorating about coming out of hibernation from long, cold winter to reclaim our yard while hanging out around a fire, usually with neighbors. The fact that we get to simply tap into a tree to harvest something that happens naturally and ends up as delicious syrup still kind of blows my mind. Plus, it is a ridiculously simple process.

If you have a maple tree (or your neighbors do), this is a free source of sweetener that is natural, local, and doesn't have to cost you much to make. We have one huge old silver maple, and typically collect sixty-plus gallons of sap from two taps. Based on the size of the tree, we could easily put in three taps, but using just two allows us to retap more on the south side of the tree where trees produce more flow.

The amount of sap that the trees give each year is dependent upon the weather. The conditions must be just right for the tree to flow; below freezing temperatures at night and above freezing during the day, with sunlight warming the tree to help increase the sap's flow. It is this freeze-thaw cycle that triggers the tree's internal pressure pumping around the sap.

If you want to geek out on botany for a minute with us . . . there are three primary processes that get sap flowing in trees: transpiration, root pressure, and stem pressure. Since transpiration happens through leaves and the sap flows before maples have leaves, it comes down to root and stem pressure. This is why the amount of sap we harvest can vary so widely from year to year. It all depends on the weather.

Generally, the tapping season will last three to six weeks. This usually begins in March for us here in Minnesota.

For those wondering if tapping the tree causes it harm, it does not. According to the Massachusetts Maple Producers Association, a healthy maple tree can be tapped for one hundred years or more! Since maples need to be at least 10 inches in diameter before tapping, it needs to grow nearly forty years before it can be tapped.

If you aren't sure what type of trees you have on your property, you can consult arborday.org/trees/whattree to try and identify the trees or reach out to your local city arborist.

Sugaring Supplies

There are many different systems that can be used for collecting maple sap, but the basic setup includes a spile, hook, and collection bucket or bag.

- **Spile:** This is a hollow metal piece that gets tapped into the tree. The tree sap flows out of the spile into a collection vessel.
- **Drill with drill bit:** Check your spile for exact sizing, but most spiles require a ⁷⁄₁₆" or ⁵⁄₁₆" drill bit. You use the drill to make the tap hole for the spile.
- **Hammer with piece of wood:** Use a hammer to gently tap the spile into the tap hole. We use a hunk of wood to place against the

spile to tap on so that we do not tap directly on the spile and deform or break it.

- **Hook (optional, depending on setup):** Hooks are either built into the spile or can be used to hang a collection vessel.
- **Bucket/bag:** This is what is used to collect the sap directly from the tree. There are lots of options for the collection vessel, anything that is food-safe, critter-proof, and covered will work. Some people cut a hole in the lid of a 5-gallon food-grade bucket and use tubing to connect the spile into the bucket. Consider the size of the vessel and weight once filled and how often you are available to empty it, knowing that some days when the sap is really flowing, a collection bag or even a large pail can overflow.
- **Pliers:** To remove the spile from the tree at the end of the season.
- **Storage buckets with lids:** To pour the collected sap into until you have enough to boil it down.

- **Cheesecloth or clean, lint-free T-shirt:** Before boiling, strain the sap through cheesecloth or a clean T-shirt to filter out bark, bugs, or anything else that may have found its way into the collection vessel.
- **Sap evaporation equipment:** The systems used for evaporating sap vary widely. Use whatever heat source gets you started; an outdoor grill burner, turkey fryer, an open fire, or build the barrel stove we show on page 108. Try different methods until you find what works best for you and your family.
- **Tree(s):** Be sure to select a tree that is healthy, without signs of insect or other damage. Size determines how many taps they can handle. A tree that has southern sun exposure is ideal. A tree that is twelve to twenty inches in diameter can support one spile, twenty-one to twenty-seven inches can support two spiles, and twenty-eight inches and greater can support three spiles.

STEPHANIE

The first couple years we collected sap, we used the sack system that Michelle does. Once we decided that this was a hobby we were going to stick with, we ordered aluminum 2-gallon buckets with lids that are specifically made for sap collection. All parts are reusable. They are lightweight and easy to remove from the spile to dump out as they fill.

MICHELLE

We've stuck with the sap sack system, which we bought when we started tapping trees over a decade ago. This includes a spile, hanger, cuff, and the blue 4-gallon 5-millileter plastic bags.

We love the ease of collecting and small storage space the equipment requires. We wash and reuse the blue bags, as they're heavy-duty food-grade plastic. Because of the design, the bags are nearly covered during collection, and we've never had issues with containments getting into the bags.

How to Tap

You'll want to drill your tap holes at about your waist height. You don't want them too high so that it is difficult to empty the filled sap collection vessels. Do not tap within 6 inches of a previously tapped hole. Drill a hole 2–2½" deep, angled upward at a 5° angle to aid with the flow of the sap. It is helpful if you add a mark on your drill bit or tape it so that you know when you've reached the desired depth. Clean out any debris inside the tap hole.

Insert the spile or spile with hook into the tap hole. Using a piece of wood as a barrier, gently tap the spile into the tap hole with a hammer. Don't hammer too hard, as this may crack the tree bark, which will cause the sap to leak out of the crack instead of down the spile into the collection vessel (been there, done that!).

Attach your collection bag, bucket, or tubing and wait for them to fill up, one happy little drop at a time. Pour sap into collection buckets and store them in a cold space until you are ready to boil. We store ours in the snow, on the shady side of our garage. It should be kept at 38°F or lower. If your sap turns yellow or cloudy, it has spoiled and should not be used for syrup making.

It takes right around forty gallons of maple sap to make one finished gallon of maple syrup. After boiling seven gallons in our turkey fryer, we will have two to three cups of finished syrup. It seems like a lot of work for a little yield, but trust me, it is so worth it.

You'll know the maple tapping season is over once the temperatures no longer cooperate, the sap becomes cloudy or yellowish, the sap changes once the tree starts budding out, or flies and other bugs find their way into sap collection buckets. Use pliers to remove the spiles.

The tree will continue to produce sap after you remove the spiles, but eventually the tap holes will heal up. There is no need to try and stop this flow; nature will take care of it. Be sure to clean your supplies well with hot, soapy water and store them away for next season. Keeping the original packaging for supplies and storing them in those helps keep them clean from dust, bugs, and debris until the following spring.

CONCENTRATING SAP THROUGH THE FREEZE-THAW PROCESS

We stumbled upon the process of freezing maple sap to condense the sugar content and fell in love. The idea is simple and comes from our local Indigenous foodways. You can capture around 80 percent of the sugar in maple sap and reduce the volume of liquid to under 20 percent of what you started within two rounds of freezing and thawing, meaning a much shorter time boiling it all down to sap. If your area gets below freezing at night, leave your sap outside. If your weather is warmer, put a bucket of sap in a chest freezer overnight.

When you freeze then thaw collected sap, the part that melts off first contains most of the sugar. If you transfer the frozen sap to a "draining bucket" (another 5-gallon bucket with holes drilled in the bottom) and let that sit at room temperature until about one third of it has melted, (it's usually ready in the evening if we take it out in the morning), that's the precious sugary portion. Toss the remaining frozen chunk of mostly ice water outside. You can put the melted sugary sap back in the freezer for a repeat freeze-thaw cycle, this time keeping the first half of the melted liquid. Make sure to label which buckets have been previously thawed if you want to do this twice. Even just fishing out any ice chunks that formed overnight will help condense that sap.

From Sap to Syrup

Our makeshift maple boiling setup worked great for years. The trick with boiling down sap with wood is to direct the flames to the bottom of the pan to boil the hottest with the least amount of wood.

Now that nature has provided all this sap, it's our job to boil it down into syrup. Do not attempt to evaporate the sap down completely in your house because it creates so much steam that no amount of ventilation can keep up. That said, boiling sap for us small-scale tree tappers is generally a two-step process:

Boil down outside: Taking the sap from, say, five gallons to under half a gallon is a good estimate for when we then bring our sap inside.

Finish off the syrup inside: This part of the process will go relatively quickly, and you'll want to watch it closely. Having the control of your stove is helpful.

BOILING DOWN OUTSIDE

You'll need fresh, clear sap and any one of the following supplies:

- Barrel stove (see project below)
- Turkey fryer with 7.5-gallon pot, high pressure propane regulator, and 20-pound propane tank
- Fire pit with grate, 1–2 large pots or steam pans, and lots of wood

DIY BARREL STOVE

"I wanted to make this because it was an inexpensive, portable, and better looking alternative to the cinder block setup we used in the past. It proved to be surprisingly efficient at boiling our sap into delicious maple syrup. Easier and faster to make than alternatives, once the fire gets going it is nearly smokeless." —Jesse (Michelle's husband)

Kits found at many local hardware stores make easy work of turning an old 55-gallon barrel into an efficient wood-fired sap evaporator. These kits will include cast iron pieces; a hinged door, legs, flue insert, and fasteners for as little as $60.

Cutting in the door.

Supplies

- 1 (55-gallon) heavy-duty barrel
- 1 barrel stove accessory kit
- Stainless steel steam/boiler pan
- 4+ feet (6" diameter) stack piping
- High temperature paint if you want a certain color

Tools

- Ear plugs and safety glasses
- Tape measure
- Level or straight edge
- Marker
- Drill/impact driver with bits to match kit bolts
- Jigsaw with metal blade

1. **Complete these steps on a level surface.** Rinse out your barrel as needed. If barrel was used to hold fuel/flammables, you must completely clean out before starting because any sparks caused from cutting steel can ignite leftover fumes inside the barrel. Dish detergent solution will neutralize oils.
2. Install door. Measure and mark the center of sealed end of the barrel. Trace the door opening, then drill pilot holes for bolts. Use jigsaw to cut along marked lines.
3. Measure a flue hole, making sure it is in line with the door so that it sticks straight up. Drill and cut flue opening.
4. Measure, mark, and fasten legs to the bottom of the barrel using pieces from accessory kit. This step will be easier if you have a removable lid–styled barrel rather than fully sealed. If fully sealed, reach through the flue hole instead of going in from the end.
5. Measure, mark, and cut out the hole for the steam/boiler pan. Match the size of hole to your pan's size, making sure the hole is not larger than the pan. This means cutting so that the barrel holds the bottom of the pan up. You want a snug fit to keep smoke from rising around the pan.
6. Install the flue insert with included fasteners. You can add high temperature sealant gasketing to better seal the flue, but it's not necessary.
7. Add stack piping to the flue insert; pressure fit should be sufficient.
8. Before you start boiling sap, keeping the steam/boiler pan full of water, start your first fire to burn off any paint. You'll need the pan inserted to get it hot enough to fully burn off paint. You can use an old grill rack in the bottom to help with air flow.

Once we have enough sap saved up to fill the turkey fryer, we boil it down. This process generally happens one to two times per week during the season. It takes half a twenty-pound propane tank to boil the sap into syrup, so we can boil down two batches with one tank. However, once the turkey fryer boils most of the water out, we do bring it inside to finish on the stove so that we can watch it closely.

Fill the turkey fryer or other boiling pot about ¾ of the way with sap. You don't want to fill it to the top, otherwise the boiling sap may splash over the edge of the pot and put out the fire. If you have more sap that can be boiled down, add it as the sap level lowers throughout the boiling process.

MICHELLE

We boil our sap with a wood fire because we enjoy it, but we've gone through a few iterations of firing; first just an open fire with a grate set on top, then cement blocks around the fire to close it in and focus the heat to the bottom of the pan, then recently my husband built a barrel stove for boiling. It was a more efficient use of wood and heated up really fast! That said, boiling all that sap down takes a full weekend or two, as we save the sap until many 5-gallon buckets are waiting.

FINISH OFF SYRUP INSIDE

- **Candy thermometer:** Once you get most of the water boiled out of the sap and it's time to finish it into syrup, you'll want a thermometer to measure the temperature. You can also use a syrup hydrometer.

- **Fine mesh sieve and/or coffee filter:** Once the syrup is complete, I line a fine mesh sieve with a coffee filter and give the syrup one last strain. There are also reusable fabric cone filters (made from wool or synthetic fibers) made specifically for maple syrup making that can be found for purchase online.
- **Large heat-tolerant measuring cup:** To collect sap during filtering.
- **Large pot:** To finish boiling inside.

Once much of the water has evaporated and gone down to about a quarter of what you began with, allow it to cool until safe to strain and carefully pour the sap through a fine mesh sieve. Transfer the strained sap into a stock pot to finish off the syrup indoors. You'll notice that the sap has turned from clear to a slight brownish or golden color at this point but that it is still watery compared to syrup.

STEPHANIE

Once sap is boiling indoors, it is very important that you watch the pot nonstop because it quickly goes from boiling sap to syrup boiling and burning all over the stovetop! I can tell that my syrup is complete by how it begins to crawl up the sides of my pot (boils and foams) and by how the consistency changes as I stir it. Big droplets form on my spoon as I test it, whereas it runs off like water when it isn't yet done. If you are not experienced yet, you can use a candy thermometer to test the syrup. You want the temperature to reach 7¼°F above the boiling point of water. This temperature will vary depending upon your elevation. You don't want to let the temperature rise above the goal temp

because it can quickly boil over and turn into sugar.

Once the syrup is complete, remove it from heat and allow it to cool slightly. Then, using a fine mesh sieve lined with either cheesecloth or a coffee filter, filter the syrup once more to remove any sediment that may have formed through the boiling process. Collect the filtered syrup in a large measuring cup or bowl. I prefer a measuring cup so that I know exactly how much syrup I made and how many jars to clean for storage.

MAPLE SYRUP STORAGE/BOTTLING

There are a few storage options. You can pour the syrup into clean jars and refrigerate for immediate use; it will keep up to a year. Or you can preserve syrup in the freezer in jars/containers filled ¾ of the way. Syrup can be kept in the freezer indefinitely. There are maple syrup bottles specifically made for syrup preservation, but please read the specific instructions that come with the bottles to determine the accurate process (varies by brand).

OTHER TIDBITS

- Always use supplies that have been thoroughly cleaned with hot soapy water when collecting, making, and storing maple syrup.
- The finished syrup color and flavor tend to increase as the season goes on. The earlier season syrup will be a light gold while the later season will be a deeper gold or even brown and the flavor will be a more prominent maple flavor.
- If you ever see mold on your syrup, discard it.
- If you want to skip the final straining of the syrup, expect that you'll see cloudy sediment at the bottom of your jars. This is not harmful but it can look unappealing.
- **Keep children and animals away from the boiling sap. Be sure to keep an eye on your boiling sap at all times and follow directions for how to use your fryer if you use this method.**

MAPLE CANDIES

The spring of 2020 was our personal best year for sap collection. The temperatures were perfect; below freezing overnight and above freezing during the day, for about six weeks. With our excess syrup, we decided to experiment with what else we could make and that's when we first made these delicious and delicate maple candies.

Since our homemade syrup is so coveted, we only make a small batch of candies. However, you can also make this recipe with purchased 100 percent pure grade A or grade B maple syrup. The grade B syrup is darker and will offer more of a maple flavor.

Yield: 1–1½ cups candies

- 2 cups 100 percent pure grade A or grade B maple syrup
- Candy thermometer
- Spatula
- Small silicone candy molds or parchment paper–lined cookie sheet

1. **Make sure that you test your candy thermometer for accuracy before beginning this project.** In a large, tall-sided pot (I use a 5-quart pot), bring the maple syrup to a boil. The goal candy temperature will change depending on altitude. Generally, you'll want to reach 27°F above boiling point of water (depending on your altitude). Once it reaches 237°F, remove from heat and cool to 175°F, then quickly begin stirring until the syrup lightens in color; this will take a couple minutes. Be careful not to splatter any hot syrup on yourself (it's incredibly painful!). Do not leave the pot of boiling syrup unattended, as it could boil over or burn.

2. As soon as it turns, quickly spoon the syrup into small silicone candy molds or pour it over a parchment paper–lined cookie sheet if you don't have molds available to you. The syrup will quickly harden so time is of the essence. Push the maple sugar into the molds if need be to obtain the detail of the molds used.

3. Once the candies are completely cooled, carefully remove them from the molds. If using a cookie sheet, you can break up the cooled candy to bite-sized pieces and enjoy them that way. Candies should be stored in an airtight container. Enjoy within 1 month. Refrigerate to extend the life of the candies.

For any hardened maple left over in the pan, you can break up and stir the mixture to create a crumble. This crumble can be used in coffee, tea, on top of ice cream, over muffins, or pretty much anything your heart desires.

INFUSED MAPLE SYRUP

Though pure maple syrup is perfect as-is, we noticed a variety of infused maple syrup hitting the market and decided to make our own—yum! For these recipes, you do not need to make your own homemade syrup, but 100 percent pure maple syrup is recommended for best flavor as the base. You'll find that it is much more cost-effective to make your own infusions, and they also make fantastic gifts. Curious how to use infused maple syrup? Well, use it as you would any regular maple syrup (on pancakes, waffles, ice cream, oatmeal, yogurt), as well as for baking, in cocktails, drizzled over proteins, blended into a salad dressing, brushed onto salmon, or splashed over roasted veggies.

Yield: 1 (8-ounce) jar

- To make my favorite infusions, apply the method below with any combination of these ingredients:
- ½ vanilla bean, slit down the center, seeds scraped out and pod included
- 2 cinnamon sticks for a light cinnamon flavor or 1 tablespoon ground cinnamon for a strong cinnamon flavor
- 2 teaspoons whole coffee beans
- 1–2 dried hot peppers of choice
- 1 teaspoon dried ginger, cardamom pods, or other dried herbs
- 2 teaspoons dried fruits and berries

1. In a medium saucepan, heat one cup of maple syrup to a low simmer and add ingredient(s) of choice. I direct you to use a medium saucepan instead of a small saucepan because the syrup tends to boil over if heated for too long or allowed to get too hot. Simmer 5 minutes, then remove from heat and allow the syrup to cool slightly.

2. Transfer the infused syrup to a clean jar. You can leave the ingredients in the syrup or strain them out with a fine mesh strainer, the choice is yours. Once jarred, wipe the rim of the jar with a dampened, clean, lint-free cloth or paper towel and again with a dry towel. Add the canning lid and tightly screw on the ring. Once the syrup is completely cooled, transfer to the refrigerator. Use within 1 year.

© *Shutterstock*

Chapter Six

HEALTHY HOME PROJECTS

Once you start realizing how easy it is to make things yourself and how much cleaner you can keep your home and your family with these products, you'll never turn back. Plus, once you find your favorite scent or flavor of something only you can make, it becomes part of your family story. Many of these recipes are mainstays in our suburban homesteads. By making our own cleaning and bath products, we save money and don't have to worry about what hidden harsh chemicals are in our products. We even have a small part in saving our planet by keeping more plastic out of landfills.

What we have available to us at a click of a button nowadays is night and day compared to even just ten years ago. When our kids were little, there wasn't much on the market for organic sprays, sunscreens, household cleaners, or lotions, so we started making our own. Here are some of our favorites that we continue to make all these years later.

Nontoxic Cleaning Items

Next time you deep clean the house, don't suffocate yourself with harsh chemicals found in commercial cleaning products. When I was a newlywed, my mom taught me about these three inexpensive, nontoxic cleaning products, and they are likely ones you already have around the house.

VINEGAR

Plain ol' white distilled vinegar, found for just a couple of bucks at the grocery store, works wonders. It might not smell good at first, but the odor quickly dissipates. Due to the level of acidity, it kills all sorts of germs and molds.

Add a tablespoon or two to each load of laundry. I pour a bit directly onto my clothes as well as into the fabric softener cartridge. Vinegar helps take the smell out of clothing and removes residue from laundry soap that may build up in the fabric over time. Running an empty cycle on your dishwasher with vinegar in the soap cartridge will also remove soap scum buildup. I do this about every six weeks or so with ours.

Wipe down your nonporous countertops and any other nonporous surfaces that need disinfecting with vinegar. Leave a dish out to eat up smells in damp, musty rooms, or to attract fruit flies if they find their way to your kitchen.

BAKING SODA

Baking soda is a great little miracle worker. I used to use a bleach powder for every tough stain on the counter that I couldn't get off with soap, but for over a decade I've just pulled out the baking soda. It's almost magical how great it is at removing all sorts of stains (including red wine!). It also removes the sticky residue that price tags leave behind on some items.

Baking soda is also a phenomenal odor eater. If my garbage can becomes smelly, I wash it out and sprinkle a little baking soda at the bottom to keep it fresh.

Instead of using harsh sprays to clean counters, just scrub with baking soda and wipe away with warm water.

LEMONS

Lemon juice is very acidic which makes it great for cleaning, and the huge perk is that it smells very fresh. Lemon juice cuts through soap scum on bathroom hardware and shower doors and it shines the metal, too! I like to dip half a lemon into baking soda and scrub my shower walls and doors with it. I let it sit on the surfaces for about five minutes and then wash it off with warm water and a sponge. You won't believe how well it works.

If you use a microwave, cut a lemon in half, and put it in a small bowl with some water.

Cook the lemon on max power for five minutes. The inside of the microwave will get all steamy, which makes wiping away any food splatter effortless.

CITRUS PEEL SURFACE CLEANER

This is another one of those "why didn't I think of that" recipes. Being able to harness the cleaning power of both citrus and vinegar together couldn't be simpler. You can use any combination of citrus in this recipe: grapefruit, lemons, oranges . . . you name it. We usually make this when we're really going through the oranges or grapefruit in late winter. That way it is ready for our spring-cleaning routine.

- Enough citrus peels to fill whatever size jar with lid that you want to infuse
- Enough white distilled 5 percent vinegar (I've tried apple cider vinegar, doesn't work as well) to cover the peels

1. Add citrus peels to a clean glass jar and cover with vinegar. Top with lid. This is a great time to use a plastic lid or a WECK jar with glass lid, as vinegar rusts regular mason jar bands. Keep in direct sunlight if possible for about 2 weeks and shake the jar at least once a day.
2. Strain the infused vinegar into a clean glass container. You can use the solution full-strength or mix half and half with water.

Use on countertops, cutting boards, sinks, and in the shower. **Never use any vinegar products on marble or granite surfaces!**

HOMEMADE BATH + BODY PRODUCTS

Once we realized that we could mix a few natural, quality ingredients and end up with superior, practical, and beautiful healing products we felt empowered. We want you to feel that power, too! As with so many homestead skills, making your own bath and body products is a simple process with a few easy steps and ingredients repeating themselves in different quantities in the recipes below.

Essential oils add another layer of healing. Look up organic oils and read about their benefits to determine which ones fit your needs. The type of carrier oil (sweet almond, cold-pressed coconut, grapeseed, jojoba, olive) you choose plays a role in the cost, healing capacity, and shelf-life. Play around with the oil blends

to figure out your mixture preference and keep notes for future reference. Some oils are oilier than others. You can choose to infuse a "base oil" to use in the following recipes or use the oils as they come. The best part of making these yourself is tailoring them to your liking! Some common, safe favorites are lavender, sweet orange, frankincense, and geranium.

STEPHANIE

Originally, we started making our own homemade lotion because the store-bought stuff just didn't cut it. Over the years I bought all sorts of different lotions, trying to find one nourishing enough to soothe my husband's irritated psoriasis and my daughter's eczema. Unfortunately, nothing lived up to the claims on the bottle. To our surprise, our homemade lotion not only nourished their skin, but also helped clear it up. We've been hooked on making our own blends ever since.

MICHELLE

I started making homemade body products as a way to use more of my garden's herbs. I loved the way this renewed an old love of herbalism and opened new doors for ways to care for my (then) babies. Knowing that all the ingredients were 100 percent natural or homegrown was so reassuring!

Making Infused Oils

We infuse oils with many different herbs and flowers to extract their natural healing traits. Once you get started, you can experiment (theherbalacademy.com is a trusted resource) and find your preferences. I tend to stick with calendula but have tried others like lavender and plantain.

This recipe is for calendula-infused oil because it is the most common base for healing

body products and is often the first one people try! Calendula flowers contain anti-inflammatory, anti-viral, and anti-bacterial properties, and have long been used to soothe skin ailments.

I love growing my own calendula for these salves, but you can make this recipe with purchased petals too, preferably from a reputable source such as mountainroseherbs.com. The varieties *Calendula officinalis* and *Calendula resina* offer the highest amounts of healing resin.

If using oils like coconut or jojoba for infusing you can infuse in the windowsill, but since I prefer olive and almond oils as my base I infuse away from sunlight. It takes a little longer, but I end up with a potent, long-lasting oil.

You'll lose a little oil in the infusion process so if you're measuring it out, add a few tablespoons to make sure you'll have enough to finish whatever recipe you're making.

Place 1 cup dried calendula petals or other herbs/petals in a pint-sized glass jar with lid. Dry petals have less chance of molding, plus the final oil will be more potent. Pour 1 cup oil (sweet almond oil and extra virgin olive oil are my regulars) over petals, making sure petals are kept under the oil (pickle pebble fermentation jar weights work well). Adjust amounts as needed. Because most of the oils I infuse are degraded by sunlight, I infuse my oils on a shelf away from direct sunlight. Shake jar every day or two, and allow it to infuse for four to eight weeks. Writing the start or end date on the jar or setting a reminder on your phone helps!

After four to eight weeks, strain out the petals using a jelly strainer bag or a fine mesh sieve. Squeeze out as much oil as you can. Store infused oils in the refrigerator until ready to use in recipes.

CALENDULA SALVE

Making salve is kind of the gateway to bath and body product making. Melt, stir, pour. It really is that simple. The oils and beeswax are both sustainable and deeply healing on their own, so being able to combine them can make just about anyone feel like a healer. **Salve is a two-step process: infusing the oil and combining the oil with other ingredients.** *You can also make it as "hard" or "soft" as you'd like by altering the amount of beeswax. A general rule of thumb is one ounce of beeswax for every one cup of oil, but you can play around with these ratios as much as you'd like.*

Supplies

- Heat-safe glass 2-cup measuring cup (note that beeswax is hard to remove completely from surfaces)
- Spoon or wooden skewer for stirring
- Small saucepan
- Noncorrosive storage containers such as 4-ounce glass jars or ½-ounce tins

Ingredients

- 1 cup calendula-infused oil, or less if adding other oils
- 1 ounce (2 tablespoons) beeswax
- 20–40 drops essential oil(s) of choice (optional)

1. Create an easy double boiler by filling a pot with water about halfway and placing the measuring cup of oils into the pan. You want the water to reach the level of the oil in the measuring cup. In a double boiler, start warming the infused oil and beeswax together. During melting, don't let the mixture get above 140°F. Try for low and slow, as going over 140°F can reduce the potency of the herbs.

2. Turn off burner and let cool slightly.
3. If adding essential oils, add just before pouring into containers.
4. Pour into smaller containers.
5. Wait until completely cooled, then add lids.

These salves will keep for 6 months. Store in refrigerator to extend shelf life.

There are many different recipes for lotion making, but here are two of our favorites. You should know that homemade lotion is much oilier than what you are likely used to, but the oils and beeswax are what lock the moisture in your skin. Because the ingredients are organic and good for your body, you will notice that your skin stays soft, moisturized, and healthy looking for much longer than it does with commercial products. Please note that a little goes a long way, so if you find it to be too oily, use less. Some favorite oils to use for lotion making are jojoba oil, organic extra virgin olive oil, shea butter, hemp seed oil, sweet almond oil, and coconut oil. Tweak to your preference.

© *Shutterstock*

- ¾ cup organic oil(s)
- 2 tablespoons organic beeswax per batch, pellets preferred
- 30 drops organic essential oil(s) (optional)

1. Mix and match your oils of choice. We recommend ½ cup organic extra virgin olive oil, ⅛ cup organic jojoba oil, and ⅛ cup vitamin E oil. Mix in beeswax. Consider incorporating infused oils (page 119).
2. Fill a small saucepan about halfway up with water and place a heat-tolerant measuring cup of oil and beeswax into the pan. You want the water in the saucepan to reach the level of the oil mixture, but not so full that it will splash all over when it's simmering. Turn up the heat to medium-high and stir the oil and wax mixture occasionally until the beeswax is completely melted.
3. Once melted, turn off the heat and use a hot pad to remove the measuring cup from the saucepan. Place the hot measuring cup on a towel-lined surface or hot pad to cool for 2 minutes. If you want to add scent to your lotion, do it now. We recommend sweet orange essential oil.
4. In a blender, add ¾ cup cold water. Turn the blender on "blend" mode and slowly pour the warm oil/wax mixture into the blender. If the blended mixture stiffens up and stops mixing, turn the blender off and use a spatula to push out any air pockets that sometimes occur during this process. Repeat as needed. Once all the oil is added to the water, set the timer for 2 minutes and blend.
5. Once blended, transfer the lotion into a clean, heat-tolerant glass jar and leave it uncovered overnight. You want to give the lotion a chance to completely cool before covering it so that condensation does not build up. The following day, cover it with an airtight lid.

If you make more than one batch at a time, store it in the refrigerator to extend its life. Since this lotion does not have any added preservatives, it will not last as long as commercially purchased lotion. Use within 1 month.

BODY BUTTER

Body butter is a more luxurious form of salve that is literally whipped into silky smoothness. I like using this body butter right after the shower as it helps lock in moisture. Body butter can be greasy but with arrowroot powder this recipe goes on smooth.

- ¾–1 cup calendula/other infusion or plain liquid oil
- ¼ cup coconut oil
- ½ cup cocoa or shea butter
- 1–2 tablespoons arrowroot powder (optional)
- 20+ drops essential oils

1. Add the calendula/other infusion or plain liquid oil and coconut oil into a heat-tolerant glass measuring cup.
2. Make a double boiler by filling a pot with water about halfway and placing the measuring cup of oils into the pan. You want the water to reach the level of the oil in the measuring cup. Turn the heat to medium and start warming all the oils and butter; low and slow is the trick here!
3. Once melted, turn off burner and, using a hot pad, remove the measuring cup from the saucepan. Place the hot measuring cup on a hot pad to cool for 2 minutes. If adding essential oils, this is the time to do it.
4. Cool in refrigerator until the edges are solidifying but not the center. You can remove and warm if it gets too cold.
5. Add in arrowroot powder if using and start whipping with a handheld mixer or transfer into a mixing bowl. Mix on high for a full 5 minutes. You'll see it start to emulsify before your eyes.
6. Transfer body butter to jars and seal with lids. *Make sure no one thinks this is whipped cream, ha!

Body butter will keep for six months, but it can melt and lose its lift. You can use it in its "salve texture" form or cool a bit and rewhip. To extend the life, store in the refrigerator.

HOT PROCESS SOAP

Making your own soap makes you feel like a true pioneer. We love this basic soap recipe as a way to quickly make more bar soap in our slow cooker. While similar to cold process soap, the hot process is more accessible, and you get to use the finished product sooner! This recipe will not yield the fancy multicolor layered soaps, but you'll end up with a great lather, scented exactly how you want—all while knowing exactly what going on your skin! Yes, there is lye in this recipe. There is lye in all true soap. Soap is made with a lye and water and fat recipe. Lye isn't scary but it does deserve respect, as it can burn skin, and shouldn't be inhaled, so we recommend mixing the lye outside while wearing glasses. Please be careful, but do not be afraid!

Supplies (it is recommended that you have separate supplies solely for soap making)

- Digital scale
- Protective gear (glasses, long sleeves, rubber gloves)
- Slow cooker (dedicated solely for soap making)
- Stick blender
- Nonmetal dishes
- Wooden spoon or rubber spatula
- Soap mold or narrow cardboard box (like aluminum foil paper) lined with parchment paper

Ingredients

- 10 ounces olive oil or sweet almond oil
- 20 ounces coconut oil (I sometimes do 15 ounces coconut oil and 5 ounces cocoa butter)
- 4.8 ounces pure lye
- 9 ounces distilled water
- Essential oils, dried petals, herbs, etc. (optional)

1. Measure out the olive oil or sweet almond oil and coconut oil or cocoa butter on a digital scale. Measure out the water into a 2-cup glass measuring cup. Get on your protective gear, then measure the lye into another glass bowl.
2. Melt the olive/almond/coconut oils either slowly in the slow cooker or quickly in the microwave (but don't boil them!).
3. Go outside or to a place with lots of ventilation because once you add the lye to water a chemical reaction releases a lot of fumes and heat. Slowly add the lye to the water and keep gently stirring until completely dissolved. **Never mix the water into the lye, as you'll waste the lye (and it will look like a middle school volcano science project and smell even worse than a middle schooler and possibly melt some things).**
4. Once the lye is 100 percent dissolved, bring it back to the melted oils in the slow cooker and slowly pour it in. Keep gently stirring.

5. Add the stick blender to the mix and blend for a few seconds, then turn off and keep mixing, then blend for a few seconds and so on. It will thicken within a minute or two. Watch for it to come to "trace," which means your soap is starting to become soap but looks like pudding.

6. Congratulations, you have done the hard part of making soap! Next, put the lid on the slow cooker and let it work its magic on low for about 50 minutes. The soap tends to "grow" with air bubbles underneath and ooze over the edge of the slow cooker in the first few minutes. While not a big deal, it's a pain to clean up so watch closely until you can stir it back down.

7. In that almost-hour, get your essential oils and other additives together. (We love blitzing oatmeal to make a gardener's hand soap for summer.) Prep soap molds by making sure they're clean. If you're using an old cardboard box like me, line with parchment.

8. Once the 50 minutes is up, test if it is done by touching a pea-sized bit to your tongue. If it zings, that's your indication that there's still more lye needing to be cooked out, so let it go another five minutes.

9. If you want to add in essential oils, dried petals, herbs, or anything, let it cool for just a few minutes, mix them in, then quickly pour into the molds, as this stuff sets up fast. Press into corners with a wooden spoon or spatula.

10. Let it set up at least twelve hours or overnight, then remove from the mold and cut into bars. You can use a crinkle vegetable cutter to add some flair.

11. Use the extra bits to make soap balls by grating soap bits, adding a few drops of water, and forming into balls.

12. This soap is also great for making back into liquid hand soap. Simply wait until cured for another day or two, then add chopped up soap to a jar of water and wait until dissolved. Transfer to a pump dispenser and you have homemade liquid soap!

TheSage.com is a great place to learn more about different oils and combinations in making soap. They also have a lye to fat calculator that helps you make your own recipes.

Making Candles

Every fall, as the temperatures begin to cool and colorful leaves begin to blanket the ground, I light up my homemade cinnamon-scented candles. The aroma is the perfect fall smell; it gets me thinking of everything fall-related: cozy blankets, home-cooked meals, warm apple cider, and the slow and dark winter that is sure to come.

I didn't learn that the majority of candles sold at big box stores are made with toxic chemicals such as toluene and benzene until a few years ago. Breathing in harmful carcinogens may increase our risk of cancer. Once I learned that, I started buying clean burning options, but they were very pricey, like $25 per small candle. That's when I decided to start making my own candles.

One hundred percent natural soy wax is a clean burning option. Additionally, soy wax doesn't produce soot while burning. I only use either soy wax or beeswax for my homemade candles and though there is an upfront cost for supplies, the overall cost per candle is extremely reduced compared to buying them. Plus, I can tailor the scents and appearance of the candles to my preference.

Once candles have been burned and only have about ¼ inch of wax left, they can be cleaned out and reused. To clean out the remaining wax, dip the emptied candle jar into a pan of hot water until the wax loosens and melts. Once the wax has melted, it can easily be dumped and wiped out for reuse.

Homemade candles aren't only wonderful to make for yourself, but they also make inexpensive

and thoughtful gifts. They can be jazzed up with ribbon or twine around the rim of the jar. Dried (pesticide-free) flower petals can be sprinkled over the hot wax after pouring to add a little beauty to the candle. Though, just a gentle sprinkle is enough because you don't want to catch the flowers on fire once burned.

DIY CANDLE

There are many ways to make candles and many different supplies that you can use. This is my preferred method for making small-batch, hand-poured candles. **Note:** *Animals can have adverse effects to essential oils, especially once the oils are heated, so please consult an expert for more info on safe essential oils for pets.*

Yield: 2 pint-sized jar candles

- Candle wicks (I prefer 8" hemp prewaxed and tabbed wicks)
- Hot glue or wick stickers
- Stirring utensil (I prefer a long wooden kebab skewer)
- Clothespins
- 4 cups soy or beeswax pellets
- Organic essential oils (optional)

1. Line your workspace with newspaper or paper towels to catch any spillover.
2. Adhere your tabbed wicks to the center of two clean, dry, pint-sized canning jars with high-temperature hot glue (it must be high-heat glue, or it will melt when burned) or wick stickers. Use a stirring utensil to push down the tabs firmly to the bottom of your jars. Thread a clothespin over each adhered wick and center it over each jar.
3. Create a double boiler by using a medium-sized saucepan. Fill pan about half full of water. In the saucepan, add a 4-cup heat-safe glass measuring cup or other heat-safe container for melting wax. Fill container with wax and warm pot to a simmer to melt wax. Once the wax has melted somewhat and made room for more wax, add more wax. You'll need about 4 cups melted wax to fill two pint-sized jars. **Different brands of wax have different instructions regarding how high to heat the wax and how low to let it cool before pouring. Please check the directions for the specific brand of wax you purchase.**

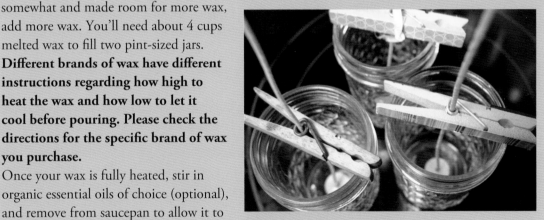

4. Once your wax is fully heated, stir in organic essential oils of choice (optional), and remove from saucepan to allow it to cool. We recommend 2 teaspoons cinnamon essential oils for a light cinnamon scent.
5. Once cooled to advised temperature, carefully pour the wax into the prepared jars, leaving 1" of headspace. Center the wick again and leave undisturbed until completely cooled. Once the wax is firm, you can trim the wick to about ¾".

FAREWELL

The future of sustainable homesteading is up to us. We hold the power in our yards, our meals, in how we garden and spend our time. Plant more food, visit farmers, pick your own berries, join a garden group, swap some seeds, or teach yourself a new craft. Learning skills that help you live your best life while helping the planet is where it's at.

FIND YOUR LOCAL HOMESTEAD HELPERS!

We believe that working together is the key to keeping homesteading sustainable. We'll leave you with one of our favorite homestead helpers, the folks at Egg Plant Urban Farm Supply. Offering supplies and classes, this place is a dream come true for budding and established homesteaders alike.

We love hearing how you guys are growing. Let's stay connected!

Websites: forksinthedirt.com + minnesotafromscratch.com

Instagrams: @forksinthedirt + @minnesotafromscratch

Facebooks: forksinthedirtmn + minnesotafromscratch

Visit us for more detailed project photos, recipes, chicken care tips, and garden inspiration!

Audrey, owner of Egg Plant Urban Farm Supply.

GARDENING RESOURCES

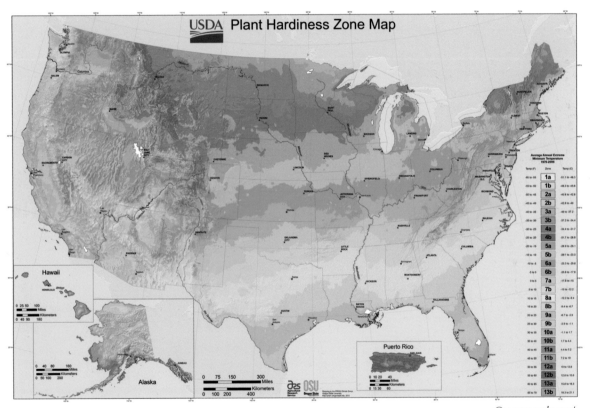

© *www.usda.gov/*

Understanding the USDA Plant Hardiness Zone Map

You can use this map as a guide for which plants are most likely to survive the winter climate in your region. Matching the right plant with your growing zone improves your chances of growing it successfully year in and year out.

So, how does this map work? The US is divided into eleven planting zones. Each of these zones is defined by their annual minimum temperature. Each 10-degree temperature difference identifies one region. Here, you'll see regions divided into "a" and "b" sections, which show each 5-degree difference. Look at plant information on plant tags or online and make sure they work for your zone.

OUR FAVORITE GARDENERS

Brie Arthur: Edible landscaping
Charles Dowding: No-dig gardening
Kevin Espiritu/Epic Gardening: General garden knowledge
Joe Lamp'l (a.k.a. Joe Gardener): All the garden knowledge
Niki Jabbour: Season extension
Meg McAndrews Cowden: Succession planting
Huw Richards: Permaculture
Jessica Walliser: General + cold climate gardening

FOOD + PRESERVATION RESOURCES

National Center for Home Preservation (http://nchfp.uga.edu): A free resource for researched-based information on approved methods of home food preservation.
Can It & Ferment It, WECK Small-Batch Preserving and ***WECK Home Preserving*** by Stephanie Thurow: Three step-by-step guides on both water-bath canning and vegetable fermentation. All easy-to-follow, small-batch recipes.
Pressure Canning for Beginners and Beyond by Angi Schneider: A trusted resource for pressure canning.
Freeze Fresh by Crystal Schmidt: A wonderful resource for freezing food.
Excaliburdehydrator.com: Excellent dehydrators and recipes for dehydrating.
Wild Fermentation (www.wildfermentation.com): Sandor Katz's website. Includes links to his fermentation books and recipes which go in-depth about the process and history of fermentation.
The River Cottage Curing and Smoking Handbook by Steven Lamb: A wonderful guide to learning how to smoke and cure meat.
The Indigenous Kitchen by Sean Sherman: A James Beard Award–winning book about cooking with Indigenous foods.
Eatwild.com: A directory to finding local food in the US and Canada.

CHICKEN-KEEPING RESOURCES

McMurrayHatchery.com: For chickens, chicken supplies, as well as other fowl.
The Beginners Guide to Raising Chickens by Anne Kuo: A great resource for beginner chicken keepers.
Gardening with Chickens + DIY Chicken Keeping by Lisa Steele.

MAPLE-TAPPING RESOURCES

Tapmytrees.com: For maple tapping supplies.

HERB + SPICE RESOURCES

Thespicehouse.com: Includes a variety of organic spices in bulk.
Mountainroseherbs.com: Bottling supplies for lotion/salve making, herbs for recipes, dried flowers, etc.
Theherbalacademy.com: For herbalism education.

ACKNOWLEDGMENTS

There are so many people along the way to thank for their help, encouragement, and support during the process of writing this book (and beyond). The knowledge we share throughout these pages comes from decades of lessons learned from generations before us, not to mention from our friends, farmers, and neighbors.

Little did I know that so many of the things that are simply second nature to my mom (and grandparents) are actually incredible tips and tricks to many others. I wasn't interested as a child, but the lessons were not lost on me, and I have been applying them at my own homestead and teaching them to my daughter as well.

I want to thank my grandmas and great grandmas for my love of gardens. Their gardens were/are filled with blooms with the likeness of a mini arboretum. Up until a few years ago, I didn't have interest in flowers whatsoever (or in vegetable gardening too much, for that matter). Maybe my newfound interest came with age, or maybe nostalgia, but I'm in the garden club now. I can't get enough. I found the inspiration and often think of their gardens from my childhood.

As always, I'm incredibly thankful for my husband and daughter and their help and patience, not just during the book writing process, but in everyday life as they assist in implementing my far-fetched ideas.

And to my coauthor Michelle, thanks so much for jumping on this crazy train with me. We've got a great yin-yang thing going on and I look forward to future collabs with you.

Stephanie

This book began and ended in collaboration with Stephanie. I can't imagine doing this with anyone else! Can't wait to see what's next . . .

Thanks to my mom and dad for instilling a deep love of nature in me, and now my boys too. I couldn't have written this book without Jesse and our boys, and all the love we've given our little homestead over the years. Cheers to my book club gals and mom friends for supporting me in all the fun ways. Thanks to Wendy (the best boss I ever quit on) and Sarah (my dear writer friend) for their robust editing chops. Kayt, you are the best idea bouncer around! Big love to my local farmers and hometown neighbors for freezing at winter farmers' markets and embracing local food, in all its forms, right along with me. This has truly been the book community built. And, for what it's worth, I'd like to thank my garden and all its inhabitants for the lessons they have taught me through the years. Let's all keep digging in!

Michelle

Michelle and I want to thank all our incredible and inspirational "featured friends" and amazing contributors featured throughout the book. We are grateful for you. We are lucky you are in our circle! Thanks for giving back, not only to us, but to all the people you help day in and day out.

And finally, we want to thank our supportive editor, Nicole Mele, and Skyhorse Publishing, Inc. for working with us on this labor of love.

Stephanie & Michelle

INDEX